PRESENTED TO

_____

FROM

_____

On the occasion of the birth of

_____

DATE

_____

Baby Lore

Baby Lore

Ceremonies, Myths, and Traditions to Celebrate a Baby's Birth

ODETTE CHATHAM-BAKER

Photographs by Christopher Baker

Macmillan Publishing Company

NEW YORK

Maxwell Macmillan Canada

TORONTO

Maxwell Macmillan International

NEW YORK   OXFORD   SINGAPORE   SYDNEY

Macmillan Publishing Company
866 Third Avenue
New York, NY 10022

Maxwell Macmillan Canada, Inc.
1200 Eglinton Avenue East
Suite 200
Don Mills, Ontario M3C 3N1

Macmillan Publishing Company is part of the Maxwell Communication Group of companies.

Library of Congress Cataloging-in-Publication Data

Chatham-Baker, Odette.
Baby lore : ceremonies, myths, and traditions to celebrate a
baby's birth / Odette Chatham-Baker ; photographs by Christopher
Baker.
p.   cm.
Includes bibliographical references.
ISBN 0-02-550665-X
1. Birth customs.   2. Birth customs—Religious aspects.
3. Lullabies.   I. Title.
GT2460.C36   1992   91-34499
392'.12—dc20   CIP

Macmillan books are available at special discounts for bulk purchases for sales promotions, premiums, fund-raising, or educational use. For details, contact:

Special Sales Director
Macmillan Publishing Company
866 Third Avenue
New York, NY 10022

10 9 8 7 6 5 4 3 2 1
Printed in the United States of America

DESIGN BY LAURA HOUGH

For my mother, Christiane

Contents

Acknowledgments

This book has grown from a steady nourishment of ideas and inspirations. It includes the knowledge of many people who have shared their family traditions with me. My heartfelt appreciation goes to all who helped:

First and foremost, Christopher Baker. He has made this book precious to me in every way. Chris's photographs reveal a sublime sense of style and beauty. From beginning to end Chris offered a steady stream of inspiration and encouragement.

My sister Lulu, who had to live with me through the creation of this book. I thank her for her patience and humor.

Ian and Alec Latimer, my sister Phoebe's children, who call me the Church Lady because I always ask about their religious endeavors, as any good godmother should. I fell head-over-heels for them when they were born and remain so.

My parents for their love, support, and strong sense of family.

Cathay Raduns for endless dinner conversations that eventually evolved into this book.

My friends Shari Rosenfeld and Olivia Crudgington for lending me their memories and souvenirs from early childhood.

Stephen Earle, who offered inspired stylish styling advice.

Beryl Milligan, who lent me encouragement and great plates.

Lyn and Jeremy Le Grice, whose stenciled home made a most wonderful first location.

All the families who lent their original birth announcements: Peter Bosch and Alison Foster, Jan and Brian Burch, Marty and Judy Fried, Anne and Kerry Raduns, Shari Rosenfeld and Yoni Barnhard, Lauren and Steven Schachtel, Joan and Brad West, and calligraphers Elaine Adler (whose beautiful birth announcement appears on p. 52) and Betsy Platkin Teutsch.

Dorothy Berlin Cummins, who compiled and translated lullabies from around the world and allowed me to reproduce some of them here.

My agent, Michael Cader, who skillfully led me through the publishing world.

Everyone at Macmillan who put their heads and efforts together to produce this book.

I also had the help of various cultural organizations, among them the Pennsylvania Dutch Folk Culture Society, Inc., the Cherokee National History Society, Inc., Inter-Tribal Indian Ceremonial Association, Independent Scholars of Asia, Inc., Father Williams of the Holy Trinity Church, London, and the cultural attachés of foreign consulates who spent long hours with me sorting out traditions and customs.

Many stores and services helped out with this book. My thanks to all who lent beautiful items for photography: in London, Tiffany & Co., the Italian Paper Shop, Designers Guild, the Monogrammed Linen Shop, Patrizia Wigan Designs, Davidoff of London, Descamps, Lyn Le Grice Stencil Designs, Ltd.; and in the United States: Leslie Allen At Home and paper white, ltd.

Baby Lore

Introduction

A birth is many things, but most of all it is a beginning. A birth marks the transition of a couple to a family, of parents to grandparents, and of older children to sisters and brothers. These family members discover, as if for the first time, that babies are magical, enchanting beings.

Naturally, traditions have developed to commemorate this arrival. The rich selection collected here is based on an international recognition of what makes a birth special. Gathered together, these rites of passage form a whole-world anthology of baby folklore. They are essentially little vignettes describing how we welcome babies into the world. This book is for romantics and for remembering.

When my nephew Ian was born, he was a first in many ways: a first child, a first son, a first grandchild, and a first nephew. We had prepared for these roles for nine months. Each of us had an idea for every decision to be made, ranging from choosing the baby's name to the format of the card that announced it. I found myself a love-struck aunt, caught up in the heady sense of romance that envelops a family rejoicing a birth. Our happy, if clumsy celebration of his birth remains a lovely memory.

Ian's birth taught me a lot about babies. Not only did I learn about changing diapers and making silly faces at two, four, and again at six in the morning, but I also found out about the heartstrings that are pulled by each little smile a baby offers. Through hearsay I glimpsed an inkling of the rich tapestry of history, mythology, and folklore that encircles the world of birth.

Some years later I was asked to be the godmother of my second nephew, Alec. I didn't quite know what that honor entailed, so I decided to do some research. At the library I discovered that the world is full of enchanting tales of baby folklore. Tattered old volumes of forgotten etiquettes are a treasure chest of ideas for the expectant family. My elder relatives also provided precious verbal histories, and a collection of old, country manners surrounding a birth.

By putting together the details we could trace of our heritage, my sisters and I were able to tailor a unique set of birth traditions to our own family's history. Our mother—part French, part Swiss, and part Scottish—grew up in prerevolutionary China; our father, an American of German parentage, was born in New York. My own childhood was spent in Japan, England, France, and the United States. As children, my sisters and I fell asleep at night listening to the myths and lore of foreign lands. Our family customs reflect our past. I have found that the sanctuary of repeated traditions, whether historical or singular to our clan, is as warming as any heartfelt vow of love.

The fruit of the womb is by nature a product of union. Two cultures merge and another is minted. Since no two families are the same, it follows that their coming together will bring a variety of cultural baggage. *Baby Lore* is about sifting through those pieces and forging family traditions of your own. A birth offers a perfect reason to take a long and loving look at your family's heritage.

It doesn't take much to encourage a family to fete a birth. In some societies an event as simple as a baby's first laugh is a cause for celebration. The formal welcoming of a child into a religious community is often the beginning of life's ceremonials. Expressed in subtleties, a ritual will often reveal a piece of its country's culture. For this reason the same ceremony varies from one region to the next. By including these regional variations in the ceremony, a family is in a sense recognizing its roots and paying homage to a whole history of tradition, using celebration as its universal language.

The traditions described in this book present a balanced blend of ancient history and modern culture. Modern adaptations have sprung from established traditions. My hope is that readers will add to the suggestions put forth in *Baby Lore* to form their own special family celebrations.

Above all, *Baby Lore* is about being swept up in the romance of bearing babies.

Odette Chatham-Baker

Paris, 1991

Baby Lore

Chapter One

Preparing the Nest

The months before birth are filled with moments of excitement and anxiety. If this energy can be harnessed to creatively pave the way for a heartwarming baby's welcome, all the better.

To a new parent, all decisions seem important. This accounts in part for the daydreaming that occupies a significant amount of time in most pregnancies. As much time may be spent trying to figure out conceivable zodiac signs as on playing with possible combinations of names.

This chapter is about imagining what your world will be like once it is filled with a new life. It contains a few of the tales and customs that parents have practiced through the ages to prepare themselves and their homes for a newborn's arrival.

Hope Bouquet

Sweet letters of the angel tongue.

JAMES G. PERCIVAL

The nuances and delicacies of language can be expressed by means far more beauteous than the ordinary written word. A "Turkish love letter" is one composed of buds and sweet scents. The language it uses is rich in subtlety. In the Middle East, where the art of florigraphy finds its roots, there were women whose sole and prosperous occupation was to decipher intricate posies. Each bud and bloom was given a specific sentiment or character trait. Considered in this light, the offering of a bouquet of flowers becomes an enchanting vehicle for extending private messages. The Victorians, often prone to using somewhat roundabout means of communication, were extremely taken with the language of flowers. The romance survives today and can be used to express a colorful array of heartfelt dreams and aspirations for the newborn baby. The Hope Bouquet is materially a medley of carefully chosen flora. In spirit it is an encoded billet-doux. Held within the bouquet are the wishes for future prosperity and harmony bestowed from parent to child. This particular choice of flowers will always have a special and private family meaning.

   Listed here are flowers with their traditional character traits. There are many books on the language of flowers that will give a more extensive and local choice.

Flower	Significance		Flower	Significance
Goat's Rue	Reason		Magnolia	Love of nature
Grape, Wild	Charity		Mimosa	Sensitivity
Hollyhock	Ambition		Mugwort	Happiness
Honeysuckle	Generous and devoted affection		Nasturtium	Patriotism
Houseleek	Vivacity		Olive Branch	Peace
Hyacinth	Sportsmanship		Periwinkle, Blue	Early friendship
Iceland Moss	Health		Rose	Love
Ivy	Fidelity		Sweet Pea	Delicate pleasures
Jasmine	Amiability		Trumpet Flower	Fame
Jasmine, Spanish	Sensuality		Tulip (variegated)	Beautiful eyes
Jasmine, Yellow	Grace and elegance		Violet, Blue	Faithfulness
Lady Slipper	Capricious beauty		Violet, Yellow	Rural happiness
Lemon blossoms	Fidelity in love		Wallflower	Fidelity in advers
Lilac, Field	Humility		Water Lily	Purity of heart
Lilac, White	Youthful innocence		Wheat Stalk	Prosperity
Lily, White	Purity, sweetness, and modesty			

A Baby's Herb Garden

Herbs that we find in our gardens today were once thought to possess mystical and potent powers. During the Middle Ages, posies and pouches of herbal cuttings were carried to ward off evil spirits. The ancient worlds of Greece, Rome, and Egypt believed emphatically in their healing powers. The Victorian era saw a penchant for floral language volumes, which included listings of herbs and their sentimental meanings. Through the ages herbs have developed a small but charming language of their own, and the herbal mystique prevails today. An enchanting forest of herbal topiaries grouped together on a kitchen sill tells a story of love and wishes. Each plant represents a simple wish or sentiment. A Baby's Herb Garden is a lovely mingling of fragrant smells and thoughts. Here is a list from which to select a harmonious grove of "little trees."

Herb	Meaning
Balm	Sympathy
Bay Leaves	Glory
Cactus	Warmth
Chamomile	Energy in adversity, love in adversity
Chervil	Sincerity
Chicory/Endive	Frugality
Convolvulus	Honesty
Coriander	Hidden wealth and concealed merit
Fennel	Worthy of all praise, Strength
Fern	Fascination
Laurel	Glory
Mint	Virtue
Myrtle	Amiability
Rosemary	Remembrance
Sage	Mutual love
Sorrel	Affection
Sweet Basil	Good wishes
Thyme	Loving remembrance

A Choice of Names

A good name is better than precious ointment
ECCLESIASTES 7:1.

Choosing a name for your child is a Herculean task. A good deal of consideration is usually allotted to this process, although in the end it may be the flip of a coin that ends a long debate. (Chapter three includes details of a Balkan naming custom. Should you be in dire despair, unable to choose between two or more names, you might turn to this method of narrowing the odds.) Bear in mind that your child will answer to the name his or her whole life long: A rose by any other name will smell as sweet, but a name can be both gift and burden.

A name is a reflection of many things. It is first and foremost an identity—in society, in geography, and in time. A name can also be a lasting link to a family's past, an expression of parental love, and a sort of talisman to invoke a rich and healthy life. Some cultures have specific guidelines to follow when choosing a name. In many instances these "rules" make the decision easier.

No Name

A child may be given any number of names, but it is generally the first, the last, and the secret or spiritual names that hold the most importance. These need not be chosen at birth. Indeed, it is still considered bad luck in many cultures to utter the child's name before some sort of purification ritual takes place.

♥ In Victorian society it was considered *de rigueur* not to utter the baby's name at all until it had been baptized. This is why many embroideries commemorating the birth of a child from that time period have the inscription Baby as the first name.

♥ The Woodland Indians of the northeastern United States carried on a community deceit before naming the child. For ten days the tribe would pretend that another woman was giving birth. Meanwhile, the mother and child would be hidden from the spirit of death. After the waiting period, the child was believed to have gained the strength to overcome the evil and could at last be named and welcomed into the tribe.

True or False Names

♥ False names are given to the newborn by superstitious parents before the formal blessing in order to trick the "angel of death." The general motive behind this custom is to save the baby from falling victim to magic spells because a charm is potent only if the true name is known. This custom explains in part our penchant for nicknames.

♥ Jewish couples sometimes call their baby Old Man until the time of the bris, in the belief that they fool the evil spirit Lilith. Lilith is constantly scouring the earth searching for

Preparing the Nest

Jewish babies. When the demon comes looking for the baby's soul, he will find, instead of young innocence, the wizened soul of a grandfather, and therefore won't be interested.

♥ Similarly, a "milk name" is given to a Chinese baby one month after its birth. False names such as Siao-Mao (Little Pussycat) or Siao-keu (Little Puppy) are substituted for real names to dupe malevolent elves into thinking the child is an animal and not worth bothering with.

♥ The Germans call a baby by a communal trick name before christening. Bohnen blättchen (Bean Leaf) and Rosen blättchen (Little Rose Leaf) are names for baby girls, and Pfannenstidche (Panhandle) is used for a boy.

♥ Ancient Egyptians held two names, a good name and a true name. The latter was carefully guarded.

♥ The Abyssinians gave the baby's true name at baptism but called the child only by its nickname. The given name was whispered in the baby's ear by his mother upon leaving the church. Likewise, a Brahman child is given two names, one for common use and the other a ceremonial name that only his father and mother know.

♥ An Apache will never reveal his name to a stranger for fear that he thus places some unfathomable strength in the stranger's hand to his own ill fortune. Similarly, Blackfoot Indians believe they would bring themselves a life of bad luck by saying their names aloud.

♥ Jewish babies born in America are given both a Hebrew name and a gentile name. The gentile name can be either a literal translation or a transliteration (one that closely resembles the euphonic cadence of the Hebrew).

Middle Names

♥ The middle name originated in Germany and is now accepted throughout the Western world. Many parents give the mother's maiden name this honor as a way of preserving ties with her family history.

Shade Names

One tradition found around the world and throughout history is that a departed soul is reborn with each baby. The child allegedly inherits the virtues of the one whose name it bears, and so it follows that the name must be selected with great consideration.

♥ The Ambo tribe of Zimbabwe gives each newborn the name of an ancestor, thus assuring protection for the baby because the *mboswa* or shade of the ancestor will look out for the child's well-being. In this way the mboswa becomes a guardian shade that brings further honor to the name. The Ambo child receives only one shade name.

♥ Many Japanese name their children for their own departed parents. They believe that departed souls await reincarnation below ground. Their patience is rewarded when they reenter the world through the bodies of the newborn.

♥ There are a few tried-and-true methods of guessing the name of the ancestor who has been reborn in a baby. One of these is to hold the baby up high as it cries. A succession of family names is then repeated until eventually the crying subsides. The ensuing calm is seen as a sign that the ancestor has been discovered, and so the baby is named.

♥ A Maori priest reads aloud a lengthy list of ancestral names. The name being pronounced as the child sneezes or coughs is immediately selected. The choice is sealed when the priest sprinkles the child with water from a small branch.

♥ A medicine man is consulted by the Yoruba tribe of western Africa before a child is given a name. The medicine man attempts to discover by means known only to him which ancestor was meant to dwell in the child. Once a name has been unearthed, the baby's face is showered with water that has sat in the shade of a sacred tree.

Do's and Don'ts of Naming Traditions

♥ In the heart of England, wise women advise against giving the same name to a child as you have given to a family pet.

♥ The Roman Catholic church prefers that a baby be named after a saint.

♥ Ashkenazic Jews believe that to name a child after a living relative will bring harm, but Sephardim Jews consider it an honor.

♥ In Greece there is quite a structure surrounding the choice of names. The firstborn son is named after the father's father, living or dead. The second son takes the name of the mother's father. A firstborn daughter bears the name of her paternal grandmother, while her younger sister is named after her mother's mother. If the honored grandparent is living, he or she should say, "I am double," after the baptism is performed.

♥ Some Greeks concur with the Ashkenazic Jews, believing that two people in the same family should not share a name.

♥ In parts of western Africa a child's name is chosen at the moment of birth. The name is arrived at by considering on which day of the week the event has occurred and the weather conditions at the time.

♥ Some parents take a literal look at their cultural heritage for a name. A name such as India, Africa, or Israel is filled with a sense of history and makes a statement of respect.

♥ Eskimos say that a person is made up of body, soul, and name, the name being the part that survives death.

Tail Endings

♥ In Great Britain there is only one person who uses a number to define her family standing. In North America a child who is named after his father immediately gains the title of junior. Should the junior's son also carry his grandfather's name, he would be the third, or III. A boy named after his grandfather, uncle, or cousin becomes the second, or II.

Recipe for a Sweet Nursery Potpourri

The very taste of a madeleine conjured up a whole childhood of memories for a Proustian hero. For some, the gentle, lingering scent of a garden potpourri possesses an equal power. However slight, an aroma has the strength to evoke a remembrance of faraway mornings spent in nursery land. Fragrant and pretty, the nursery blend is simply a mix of petals, leaves, and fruit collected in an ornamental container. A bowl mounded with pale rose petals and curls of orange and lemon peel is a glorious feast for all the senses. Three times a year, scatter a few drops of rose and jasmine oils over the potpourri and turn it lightly. In this way the aroma is refreshed, and the strength can be adjusted to suit one's taste. The recipe below will make about one pound of sweet-smelling potpourri.

One golden rule for making a dry potpourri is to be certain that all of the dried ingredients—flower heads, petals, herbs, and leaves—are bone-dry before starting. If mildew occurs, it is best to toss and start again from scratch.

❦ ❦ ❦ ❦ Ingredients for a Dry Potpourri ❦ ❦ ❦ ❦

3 ounces whole tulips (pale yellow or the palest pink)
4 ounces mixed rose petals (yellow or pale pink, and white)
3 ounces curled lemon peel
3 ounces curled orange peel
2 ounces whole lemon verbena leaves
1 ounce powdered orrisroot
10 drops jasmine oil
6 drops rose oil

❦ ❦ ❦ ❦ ❦ ❦ ❦ Utensils ❦ ❦ ❦ ❦ ❦ ❦ ❦ ❦

Wooden mixing spoon
Large ceramic mixing bowl
Large brown paper bag lined with wax paper
Glass eyedropper for oils
2 wooden clothespins

In the ceramic mixing bowl, stir together the flowers, citrus peels, and leaves. Sprinkle on the orrisroot powder and stir once more. Sprinkle the drops of jasmine and rose oils over the ingredients and toss gently to season. Next, pour the mixture into the lined paper bag. Fold over the top and secure with clothespins. Curing the potpourri takes a full two weeks. Place the bag in a dry, shady, cool spot. Every three days, open it up and turn the ingredients carefully with a wooden spoon. The contents are now fit to be called a potpourri. Pour a pretty bowlful and embellish it with a few dried rosebuds on top.

Monday's Child

A child's time and day of birth is often regarded as an omen of things to come. In the Far East, a baby's horoscope is cast based on the precise hour and date of birth. Any child born in Europe or North America is bound to hear the predictions of the "Monday's Child" poem.

Monday's child is fair of face,
Tuesday's child is full of grace,
Wednesday's child is full of woe,
Thursday's child has far to go,
Friday's child is loving and giving,
Saturday's child works hard for its living,
And the child that is born on the Sabbath day
Is bonny and wise, and good and gay.

And a lesser-known German version:

Monday's child, pretty child,
Tuesday's child dances quickly,
Wednesday's child doesn't like standing,
Thursday's child has far to go,
Friday's child I like very much,
Saturday's child works hard,
Sunday's child sings so fine,
Would like to be with you.

Some Other
Birthtime Beliefs

♥ A chime baby: One born between the stroke of midnight on a Friday and first light on Saturday is said to be blessed with second sight.

♥ Among the Basques, a chime baby is one born at the chime of four, eight, or twelve bells. This baby, too, has the gift of second sight.

♥ To be born on Christmas day itself is considered extremely lucky in England and France.

♥ Babies born with the new moon will be eloquent speakers; those who arrive during the last quarter will be good reasoners.

♥ In France, birth during the moon's increase is said to produce a fast grower.

♥ The sage of a family will be the third son, but the seventh child of a seventh child is destined for a life of luck.

♥ In northern England, a child born on Sunday is said to be free from the grasp of evil spirits its whole life.

♥ It is said in North Carolina that any baby born in March will be fickle.

♥ In the Carolinas it is said that a baby born on the twenty-sixth of any month will become very, very rich.

Birthflowers

Month		Flower
January	The progressive buddings of different flowers through the year	Carnation
February	make up a kind of natural calendar. Each month has its own	Violet
March	birthflower. It is common that a new mother is given a bouquet	Hyacinth or Grape Hyacinth
April	of her child's birthflowers as a gesture of best wishes and good	Sweet Pea
May	luck. We live in varied climates, and so the birthflowers differ	Lily of the Valley
June	from country to country. The ones cited here are from New	Rose
July	England. If these flowers do not coincide with the natural calendar	Delphinium
August	of your area, a book on local flora may list alternatives.	Gladiolus
September		Aster or September Aster
October		Marigold
November		Chrysanthemum
December		Narcissus

Birthstones

As with birthflowers, each month has its own birthstone. Legend has it that if the stone is worn by children born in that month, they will have good luck. Many parents select a couple of beautiful gemstones for their child at birth. When the child celebrates his or her sixteenth birthday, the stone is set in a piece of jewelry. Cuff links, earrings, and key rings are the obvious choices. This gift makes a lovely investment of love and pride, to be used and cherished through life.

January   Garnet (Constancy)

February   Amethyst (Sincerity)

March   Aquamarine or Bloodstone (Truth)

April   Diamond (Innocence)

May   Emerald (Happiness)

June   Pearl or Moonstone (Health)

July   Ruby or Carnelian (Love)

August   Sardonyx or Peridot (Felicity)

September   Sapphire (Wisdom)

October   Opal or Tourmaline (Hope)

November   Topaz (Fidelity)

December   Turquoise or Zircon (Success)

Preparing the Nest

Signs of the Zodiac

Invented by the Babylonians in the third century B.C., astrology is a science based on the intricate study of the stars. Astrology has been looked to by many cultures around the world for advice and direction.

Many Far Eastern societies still cast a child's horoscope as soon as it is born. The Singhalese culture of Sri Lanka calls for an astrologer to select a name for the infant, derived from the name of the ruling planet at the moment of birth. This name is like the Chinese "milk name": The astrologer whispers the name to the father who whispers it in the baby's ear. It is never mentioned aloud in case evil spirits should use it to cast their spells. In Vietnam the successes and failures in a child's life are mapped out by an astrologer at birth.

Today, many look to the zodiac to determine how the course of their lives and their children's will run. These are some of the better-known positive and negative character traits of the signs:

Capricorn *(December 22–*
January 20) The Goat
Faithful and constant;
grumbling and
unapproachable.

Aquarius *(January 21–*
February 18) The Water
Bearer
True in friendships,
innovative at work; but can be
opinionated and distant.

Pisces *(February 19–March*
20) The Fish
Gentle and supportive; insecure
and dreamy.

ries *(March 21–April 20)*
The Ram
Highly enthusiastic and
competitive; selfish and
stubborn.

Taurus *(April 21–May 21)*
The Bull
Persistent and constant, but
slightly lackadaisical and a
plodder in work.

emini *(May 22–June 21)*
The Twins
Communicative and active;
superficial and obstinate.

Cancer *(June 22–July 22)*
The Crab
Sensitive and caring; defensive
and possessive.

Leo *(July 23–August 23)*
The Lion
arismatic and organized in
dership; insecure and bossy.

Virgo *(August 24–September*
22) The Maiden
Creative yet modest; tends to
be disorganized and highly
critical.

ibra *(September 23–October*
23) The Scales
Diplomatic and romantic;
resentful and vain.

Scorpio *(October 24–*
November 22) The Scorpion
Loyal and energetic; aggressive
and secretive.

Sagittarius *(November 23–*
December 21) The Archer
Adventuresome and open;
blunt and restless.

Chapter Two

Old Wives' Tales

Children are a staircase to Paradise
PERSIAN PROVERB

Old wives' tales are myths and superstitions that have been passed down from one generation to the next. The origins of most folk beliefs are unknown or obscure. Nonetheless, many of them have become as established a part of birth observances as knocking on wood is for luck. Superstitions are sprinkled throughout our daily speech and actions, and so it is hardly surprising to find a large number of them surrounding the birth of a child.

The customs differ from one region to another, some even contradicting one another. However, they seem to fall into specific categories that reveal our natural fears and curiosities. A common concern around the world is luck. It seems that parents will stop at nothing to ensure that their child will be clothed with a blanket of lifelong good fortune. Everything from throwing money into a child's first bath to climbing up ladders has been performed in the name of luck. Wicked fairies are also a cause of parental

Old Wives' Tales

concern. They seem to have a worldwide reputation for stealing vulnerable young babies. According to baby folklore, certain precautions will thwart this quest. Many also swear by tried and perhaps true methods of guessing the sex of the child before it is born.

The stories and wise sayings are not just for the superstitious. They voice an interesting narrative of birth tradition. Each of these legends should be taken with a grain of salt, so to speak. You may find yourself unconsciously pressing a silver coin into the palm of a baby's hand or planting an ash branch over the nursery door, just in case.

Predictions

Before the advent of the sonogram, there were other, somewhat less precise ways of telling the sex of an unborn child. Even if you do know the gender of your baby through scientific means, it might be fun to try these well-worn tales that have even persisted during these times of electronic precision.

- ♥ If the expectant mother carries high, a boy will be born; if she carries low, a girl.

- ♥ Offer the unassuming mother-to-be the simple choice of a lily or a rose. Should she choose the rose, a girl will be hers; the selection of the lily foretells the birth of a boy. This test dates back to medieval times.

♥ In parts of northern Greece, a pair of scissors and a key are placed on separate chairs. The pregnant woman is then brought in the room and is asked to sit down. If she chooses to sit in the chair with the scissors, she will bear a girl; if she gravitates to the chair with the key, this indicates she will have a boy.

♥ Expectant parents wanting to know the gender of their baby before it is born should sleep with a piece of fresh horseradish underneath their pillows. Upon waking, both should check its color. If the mother's horseradish is tinged with black, the baby will be a girl; if the husband's morsel turns dark first, a boy will be born to them.

♥ One of the more obscure methods of prediction: The Wai-Wai Indians of Guiana closely examine the activities of the common woodpecker for signs of whether the child will be male or female. If the woodpecker whistles, the mother will bear a boy; if the bird is tapping, expect a girl.

♥ In parts of England, the test is as follows: Hold a piece of cotton over the stomach of a pregnant woman. If the cotton moves back and forth, she will have a boy; if the cloth hangs straight and motionless, she will bear a girl.

♥ The Tacama Indians of Bolivia used a type of dream analysis to figure out what sex their child would be. If both parents dreamed of a round object, such as a round fruit, then the baby would be a boy. If they dreamed instead of a long object, such as a banana, then they would have a daughter.

♥ An Aztec formula that a number of Manhattan obstetricians

swear by goes as follows: Note the age of the mother at the time of conception, then note the year of conception. If both are even or both are odd, a girl will be born. If one of the numbers is even and one odd, then a boy will be born. For example, a woman who conceived at the age of twenty-nine in 1991 will have a girl.

♥ A female child will be born if the mother has satisfied her craving for sweet things during her pregnancy.

Just for Luck

Some of the most endearing folk-beliefs are about luck. Whether or not they believe in the power of good-luck superstitions, many people perform lucky rituals just in case.

♥ *Carry the baby upstairs before you carry him down because if his first journey in life is upward, he will rise in the world. Although originally meant for a home birth, this condition can be fulfilled just as well in a hospital setting. Make the baby's first journey by stepping up onto a box or stepping stool while you are carrying him.*

♥ *A baby who cries at a christening will have good luck. Many a godparent has gently pinched a godchild while standing at the baptismal font.*

♥ *A large number of hazelnuts harvested means that many babies will be born during the coming year. (England)*

♥ *In Bavaria a baby's financial success is assured if the baby's first bath contains a gold coin.*

♥ *According to a Greek tradition, if the father puts a pinch of salt in the baby's bath three days after birth, the child will grow up to be witty.*

♥ *A child will become very wealthy if the initials of his full name spell a word. (Southern United States and Herefordshire, England)*

Tiny Telltale Signs

Often when a child is born its parents examine its features and behavior for signs of what the child will be: lucky and generous? thieving or stingy? These are a few tales to go by:

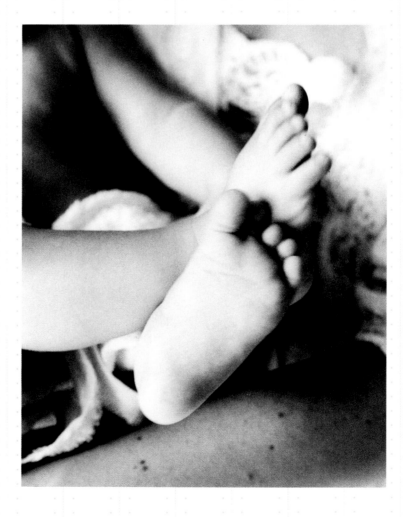

One Arab folk belief is that if a baby is born with an unusually long umbilical cord, the child will have an unusually high intellect.

♥ *In the Middle East a child born with a birthmark on the sole of the foot will grow up having a strong character.*

♥ *An American superstition says that older parents bear more intelligent children.*

♥ *A navel that sticks out is a sign of luck in life.*

♥ *If a baby has large ears, it will be a loving, giving person, but if it has small ears, it will be stingy.*

♥ *Children born with hairy arms are headed for a prosperous life.*

The Basques predict that a child born with fists tightly clenched will be a miser. In Virginia and the Carolinas, a child born so will grow up to be a thief.

♥ *In the north of England, it is said that babies born with large ears are born lucky.*

♥ *A child born with a dimpled chin will be wealthy.*

♥ *Babies born with open hands will be generous.*

♥ *Bald-headed babies are destined to be bright students.*

♥ *A baby born with a large, wide mouth will be a good singer.*

♥ *A birthmark found in the upper part of a baby's body means it will enjoy success in life.*

Admonitions

Old wives' tales are full of wise sayings and words of warning for expectant parents to heed. These are a few for the superstitious to consider.

- ♥ Do not purchase a baby carriage until the baby is born. If you do, you might be tempting Providence.
- ♥ An owl who sings in the woods is announcing to all that there is a woman nearby who is pregnant but does not know it. (Basque)
- ♥ A pregnant woman handling weapons in Tibet will produce a child with a birthmark.
- ♥ In Tibet a child of seven or eight who is losing his teeth is taught never to show the gaps to a pregnant woman. If he does, the unborn baby will steal the incoming teeth before they surface, and the gaps will not be filled until after the baby is born.
- ♥ If an infant's cradle is not paid for in advance, he or she will grow up poor. (Scotland)
- ♥ All knots should be untied at the hour of birth in order to speed an easy delivery. (Germany, Ancient Rome, India, Lapland, Australia, Bulgaria)
- ♥ Open all locks and doors during labor. (Greece)
- ♥ Many consider it bad luck to rock an empty cradle.
- ♥ Never leave the bed linens and clothes of the mother and

newborn outdoors at night. Any object exposed to the stars may carry the spell of the evil eye. (Basque)

♥ Do not sweep a room while a baby is asleep. If you do, the "dream soul" that leaves the body during sleep will be swept away with the dirt. (Africa)

♥ Do not name the child after a favorite animal. (Herefordshire, England)

♥ If the godmother is made to look behind her on the way to the baptismal font, the child she is holding will be tearful its entire first year. (Basque)

♥ A godfather who recites the creed badly during the christening ceremony will cause his godchild to be crooked. (Basque)

♥ It is bad luck to put a baby's dress on over its head. Instead, pull the garment up from the waist until the first year has passed. (American)

♥ Do not trim a baby's nails before it is a year old (you can bite them instead), or it will grow up to be a thief.

Protective
Precautions

Many parents fear that malevolent fairies will steal their babies away. A multitude of safety measures have evolved from this fear.

♥ After the baby is born, it should be rocked in its cradle all night long in order to prevent a devil's abduction. This practice should continue until the child is baptized. (Greek)

♥ When a child is born, the Chinese tie some coins together with a red string for it to wear. The coins act as an amulet that ensures a rich and healthy life for the child.

♥ The Chinese also tie bells to their children's wrists or ankles to scare off evil spirits.

♥ In Yugoslavia a bell is attached to the cradle arch for the same purpose.

♥ Shells are one of the oldest known protective amulets. Greek islanders tie a string of these to the cradle for protection against sinister fairies.

♥ A follower of Manx folklore would put a pair of the father's trousers across the baby's cot so that fairies would be frightened away.

♥ In England it was the custom to place a piece of the father's clothing in the crib so that a child would have an instant connection with him. Should the garment be red, all the better because it would also serve as a protection from evil.

♥ In Italy the father's nightshirt is placed in a baby's cot.

♥ A piece of the father's wardrobe placed in the vicinity of the cradle would be protection enough to guard the Scottish "bairn."

♥ In the south of China, a word-charm is pinned to a pair of the father's trousers, which are then placed near the child's bedstead. In this way the parents can be certain that the baby will not be harmed because all evil will pass into the word-charm.

♥ In Sarajevo, Yugoslavia, a piece of paper on which is written a warning against witches is sewn into the hem of a baby's clothes.

♥ An amulet is put on a child taken outdoors before baptism in northern Greece. It consists of a piece of the Good Friday Eucharist, a prayer against the Evil Eye, and a piece of thunderstone.

♥ Evil fairies who are trying to steal the baby from its cradle will be thwarted by a Bible placed in the crib, and loose salt and iron objects strewn around the crib.

♥ In India an iron knife is hidden under the bed immediately following birth, to protect the mother and child from spirits.

♥ In Greece a pair of scissors is placed in or under the bed for protection. A broom or a piece of leavened bread imprinted with the sign of the cross will serve the same purpose. The Greeks also protect all windows by hanging over them little crosses fashioned of cane.

♥ The Pennsylvania Germans used a *rooke shtae* (rest stone) to calm a fretful baby. A stone from a stake fence was placed under the cradle and was thought to invite peace and rest.

♥ According to Basque tradition, the cradle must be rocked all night long so that the Devil cannot snatch the baby away. Wheat and money must be left on the windowsill of the baby's room for the same reason.

♥ A Scottish fisherman used to hang his nets over the curtains so that his baby would not be abducted by fairies. The nets would stay there until the child was baptized.

♥ It is both a Welsh and a Jewish superstition that bits of red ribbon or red string be tied to the cradle for protection.

♥ Pliny, a Roman historian of the first century, recorded that a child given the gift of coral would be safeguarded against bewitchment, so a coral amulet was worn. The "coral and bells" that made up Victorian teething rings served the same purpose. Red coral was believed to be especially potent against evil. A teething ring was formed of a red coral band to which silver bells were attached. The jangling of silver bells was supposed to scare away the fairies, which is why baby's rattles are often made of silver and make noises when shaken.

Professions

A parent wishing to second-guess her baby's future profession has only to follow one of these country customs. The glories of the farmyard, college campus, and Wall Street are foretold.

♥ *A Pennsylvania Dutch custom is to place a baby who is able to crawl on the floor in front of three objects: a Bible, a potato, and a bottle. If the child crawls toward the potato, he will be a farmer; toward the Bible, a preacher; and toward the bottle, alas, a drunk.*

♥ *Place some feathers near a baby. If the baby notices them and tries to grab them, he or she will keep a clean house. If the baby ignores the feathers, he or she will be messy.*

♥ *Navajo Indian parents have been known to bury a small piece of their baby's umbilical cord near something they wish to affect their child's future. Many such secret burials take place near banks, oil wells, and rodeo arenas.*

♥ *Another American test is to put a baby in front of a coin, a potato, and a book before it has reached its first birthday. If the potato is chosen first, the child will become a farmer; if the baby reaches for the coin, the child will be a financier; and if the baby chooses the book, he or she will become a scholar.*

♥ *A Bible, a silver coin, and a deck of cards are other choices. The first indicates a preacher has been born; the second, a child destined for riches; and the third, the life of a gambler.*

♥ *In China, a child who grabs hold of a flute will be a musician; a pen means a writer has been born; a brush indicates a painter; and scissors mean the child will be an expert tailor.*

Baby Lore

Sacred Plants

The mythologies of ancient Rome and Greece are laced with myths of spirit trees and sacred plants. The lore of birth is also filled with stories of the magical powers of Nature. According to Norse mythology, the first man was born of the ash, and the first woman of the elm. The god Adonis sprang from a myrrh tree. Old sayings from around the world imply that cradles bring luck and protection if they are constructed of a particular type of wood. Amulets and talismans of various seeds and tree barks are also supposed to provide immunity from noxious nursery spells. These are just a few of the superstitions surrounding birth and plant lore.

Christmas Roses

In rural England many doorways are graced with a Christmas rosebush planted on either side. The threshold is known in witchery to be a weak spot, and the presence of this plant protects it from any harmful fairies who might try to enter the house and steal a newborn baby.

Cinnamon

In the province of Westphalia in Germany, children leave grated cinnamon bark on the windowsill in order that a sister or brother will be born soon.

Fennel

To scare witches away from the children's room, hang a bunch of fennel in the doorway.

Garlic

Pungent, redolent garlic is hung near the nursery window by the Basques to keep evil spirits at bay. In Greece, too, a baby is adorned with a necklace of garlic after birth or after baptism. The Portuguese sew bits of garlic into the hems of a baby's clothes as a charm against evil.

Mistletoe

Lay a sprig of mistletoe in a newborn's cradle, and it will keep the child out of fairies' reach.

Peony Seeds

An amulet of peony seeds was once placed around the necks of young children. With this protection the children were safe from the powers of wandering witches.

Primroses

According to a Somerset legend, if thirteen primroses are placed beneath the cradle before it is occupied, the newborn will be safe from bewitchment and fairies.

Rue and Rosemary

Rue and rosemary are often fastened to the cradle by the Portuguese to avoid bewitchment.

Sacred Woods

♥ In northern Europe the most sacred of all trees is the ash. Norse legend has it that mankind sprang from a twig of this tree. This was the wood that Cupid chose to make his arrows, and Achilles his spear. A baby born in Devon was first bathed before the heat of an ashwood fire. The Scots tie ash twigs in a bundle and hang them from a baby's cradle arch for safety. Cradle rockers made of ash or mountain ash (rowan) protect a baby's innocence. Some English mothers would rock their babies in a hammock tied to an ash tree, believing that no animal or evil would come near.

♥ In the Balkans cradles made of the following woods were considered protective: hazel, yew, oak, and hawthorn.

♥ In Japan the wood of a peach tree is used to make protective amulets. The Chinese also revere this wood and believe children to be safe under its shadow. It is still believed by some that ruinous demons use small children to reinforce the foundations of a bridge. Such is the power of the peach tree that if a child should wear an amulet made of its wood, the demons would never dare come close. Peach wood arrows are formed and attached to a baby's cradle. The cradle is also made of peach wood, T'ao-shu, as a charm to ensure a long life. Sung-shu, or pine, is a good wood to use for a baby's cot. This tree is a lucky one in China and is thought to give a child a good start toward an admirable life.

♥ Crosses made of yew are tied to the cradle of a Croatian new-born. Yew is considered a sacred tree in many Slavic countries. The Croatians also attach bunches of ivy berries to the arch of the cradle. The combination of wooden crosses and berry branches is said to deter evil spirits.

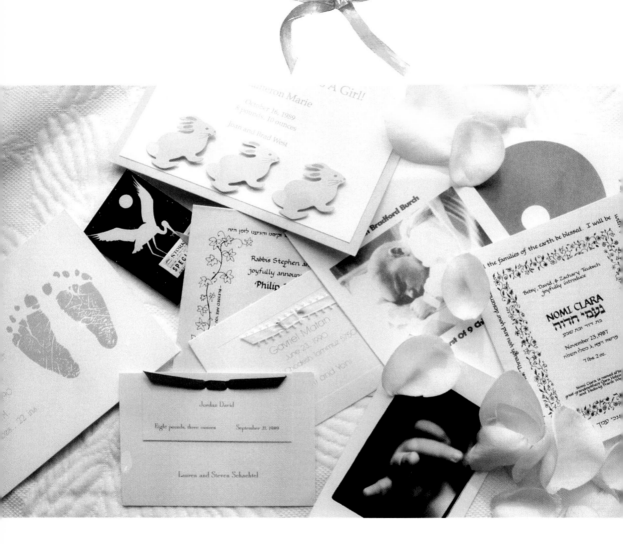

Chapter Three

Announcements

Chapter three is rich in fact and fiction. It presents the myths, oddities, and conventional methods of announcing a birth. There are many beautiful ways of expressing the joy and pride that accompany a baby's arrival. An announcement recounts the particulars of this rejoicing and allows others to join in. Generations of imaginative parents have refined the art of announcing a birth into a micro-culture. Some are sophisticated and tasteful while others retain the charm of time-worn country customs.

Tidings of birth do not have to be proclaimed on a card. Announcements can take the form of a colored blanket hung out for the neighborhood to see. A stenciled nursery announcement is a private family one, in the oldest of Swedish traditions. The wall stencil placed above the newborn's bed will last well through childhood. An announcement made in a newspaper is there for all to share. The Victorians came up with a few sly ways of announcing a birth to older siblings without ever mentioning the issue of sex. A stork's annual spring migration offered a convenient explanation of a baby's arrival.

The Rules of Announcement

There are no hard-and-fast rules for birth announcements. The formal proclamation usually notes the baby's name, the parents' names, the date of birth, and the weight of the baby. Anything included after that is up to you.

The announcements can be engraved, printed, handwritten, or professionally written in calligraphy. The choice of birth announcements is usually made before the event. A style of card is selected, the format decided on, and all the known particulars given. When the baby is born, a phone call to the stationers is made with the exact spelling of the child's names along with the other details to be printed. Many parents make a mailing list for the announcements before the baby is born. All of these preparations save precious time and energy later.

You may choose to give your announcement a humorous note (for example, "After nine months, we had a 9-pound 11-ounce baby boy on February 9, 1990—Kevin Bradford Burch—our first of nine children") or use it as a way of including older siblings in the celebrations (for example, "Sally and Daniel Moore join Matthew in joyfully announcing the birth of his sister, Sophie Marie, on September 22, 1990, 7 pounds 10 ounces"). If a child has been named for a relative, an explanation can be added to the announcement ("Sophie is named for her great-grandmother and her aunt Marie"). There is also an extensive range of printed announcements that offer a faster, less expensive alternative. These only need to be filled in with the baby's particulars and sent on their way.

The Formal Announcement

A small card is fastened to a larger one with a ribbon of either pink, blue, or white. The smaller card is centered against the top edge of the bigger one. The first and middle names of the newborn are engraved on the miniature card, along with the weight and date of birth. The larger card holds the names of the parents.

Paul Henry

Eight pounds three ounces   October 21, 1990

Katherine and Martin Cooke

Another version of the formal announcement has two cards as before. The little one, bearing the first name, middle name, and date of birth, is centered on the larger white card. A pale blue or pale pink ribbon ties it to the folded, larger card. The writing inside the card may read:

Ron and Mary Brown
are very happy to announce
the birth of their son

9 Scott Street
Fairfax
California 94930

The Jewish Announcement

In a Jewish birth announcement, the traditional inclusion of the baby's and parents' names, date of birth, length, and weight remain the same. It is the addition of the baby's Hebrew name, however, that pronounces the parents' pride of Jewish heritage. The Hebrew name is written in either Hebrew letters or their western transliteration. Some parents prefer to give both. The birth date is given according to the Gregorian and lunar Jewish dates. It is also nice to let people know if the baby was born on the Shabbat (the Sabbath), at the dawn of a new moon (Rosh Chodesh), or during a Jewish holiday. This information can be noted beside the birth date.

Gavriel Matan
June 23, 1990
Rosh Chodesh Tammuz 5750

Shari Rosenfeld and Yoni Barnhard

The Postcard Announcement

The larger photographic supply stores carry special print papers with "Postcard" and a space for a mailing address inscribed on the back. These can be cut into individual cards and printed with a black-and-white image of a baby's face, hand, or foot to make wonderful announcements. Another homemade and creative touch is the addition of a rubber stamp imprint telling of a baby's name and date of birth. This is applied to the back of the card, opposite the mailing address.

The Family Tree
Announcement

| Samuel Zoller | Mollie Berlin | Joseph Parnes | Pauline Hollis | Max Sadler | Angie Cohen | George Gerber | Rose Goldberg |

Arthur Zoller · Miriam Parnes · David Sadler · Shirley Gerber

Kenneth Zoller · Patricia Sadler Zoller

Amy Susan Zoller

דודה שושנה

born January 19, 1989 · 8 pounds, 10 ounces

"she is our beloved"

A family tree announcement is one laden with the twists and turns of a family's social history. It can tell as much or as little as you like. Some parents choose to concentrate on the immediate family, giving only the names of the child's parents, grandparents, and great-grandparents. This information is sufficient for an announcement. If this is to become an ongoing family project, however, you will need to gather more details from existing family records or from older relatives.

The tree itself can be drawn freehand or in a strict linear design. If they are to be sent only to the closest family members, they can be handmade. Otherwise, a printer can copy your design.

On a Bed of Damask Roses

A box wrapped in plain brown paper and tied with rough garden twine seems a very discreet way to announce this new and magical part of your life. However, mind the adage, "Never judge a book by its cover," for in this case it will serve you well.

This is a birth announcement that finds its charm in contrasts. Plain on the outside, it is baroquely splendid once unraveled. A pretty box is fastened with a lash of diaphanous gold ribbon. Its contents betray themselves before opening: a fragrant bed of dried damask roses. Waiting to be read is a small card revealing the name, date of arrival, and weight of the newborn. Written in calligraphy on a hand-torn piece of Italian paper or printed on a thick ivory card, this announcement is one to be cherished—a secret pearl in its oyster.

I love the idea of discovering layers of joy—the box, the card, and the roses. It heightens the moment and therefore your joy of announcing a birth to those far away.

Newspaper Announcements

A newspaper announcement proclaiming a birth to the general public appears in the Births column of the personals section. A national or local newspaper is usually contacted by either a telephone call or a letter. There are a few guidelines to follow when placing this announcement. Simple, spare wording is generally used. The information listed in this far-reaching announcement is the family name, which will appear in bold capitals, followed by the date of birth, the first names of the parents, and the name of the newborn with the word son or daughter preceding it. Optional additions include the mother's maiden name placed in parentheses and preceded by the word née; the name of the hospital where the birth took place; the town of birth; and possibly the names of older brothers or sisters who also welcome the baby.

A Few Examples

If the mother, Sarah Smith, has kept her name after marriage but the child bears her father's surname, Jones, the listing will read as follows:

JONES—On July 18, at Marin County Hospital, to Sarah Smith and James, a daughter, Mary Alice.

LATIMER—On April 27, in Rolling Hills, California, to Phoebe (née Heideman) and Mark, a son, Alec Tristan, a brother for Ian.

JENKINS—On September 7, to Charlotte (née Brooke) and Timothy, a daughter, Emma Brooke.

ROTHSTEIN—On June 21, at the Albert Einstein Hospital, New York, to Sharon and Jacob, a son, Daniel Abraham.

CRUDGINGTON—On August 19, to Susan and James, a son, James Crudgington, Jr.

WILLIAMS—On December 19, to Cathy and Steven, a son, Kenneth Neil, a grandchild for Ruth and Kenneth, Lily and John McBride.

RADUNS—On February 28, to Anne and Kerry, Jenna Stephanie, a granddaughter for Barbara and Ed.

Handing Out Cigars

The origins of this funny birth custom are vague. There are some who say it comes from the American Indian "potlatch" custom, the ritual of sharing one's happiness with the tribe. The act of collective celebration allows the fortunate individual to avoid the jealousy of others. The practice of handing out cigars may also derive from an ancient Mayan tradition of puffing on lighted tobacco firebrands to please the olefactory senses of the gods.

Whatever the origins, the custom survives today as a proud gesture that a baby has been born. The happy distribution usually takes place at the hospital, immediately following the birth. The newborn's father comes prepared with a small stockpile of choice cigars that he passes out to visiting family, friends, and even strangers who share in his excitement of new parenthood. Any cigar will do; however, many select a box of the best because this occasion is to be savored and long remembered.

Announcements

A Nursery Announcement: Swedish Name Stencil

An old Scandinavian custom welcomes a baby into the nursery. The Swedish painter Carl Larson beautifully illustrated the tradition of inscribing the name or initial of the child above its sleeping place. This charming practice both welcomes the child and gives it its rightful place in the family and home. Essentially a nursery announcement, it acknowledges that a new member has joined the brood.

Lyn Le Grice, who created the name stencil scheme shown opposite, laced a simple pattern of leafy green branches around the name. This motif extends around the ceiling of the room, giving the child a peaceful scene to gaze upon as he or she drifts off to sleep.

Many of us live less than stationary lives. An alternative to the name stencil permanently painted on the wall is one that is hung as a painting. The design can easily be applied to a stretched canvas or a prepared wooden board. The stencil design can also decorate a painted box or chair, to form a child's trousseau. These wonderful keepsakes will no doubt be treasured by children and grandchildren in the future.

Colorful Birth Tidings

In the oldest of societies around the world, color has played quite a significant role in birth announcements. The traditional uses of color in birth tidings endure as unspoken announcements to the neighborhood.

A crown of green olive branches adorned the doorway of a newborn boy's home in ancient Greece. Strands of pure white wool looped above the front door to announce the birth of a female baby.

It was the habit of nineteenth-century German aristocrats to bring the news of a birth to the household staff by means of a beribboned bunch of flowers called a *Freudemaien*. A bouquet tied with a red ribbon told of the birth of a boy; a white ribbon heralded a girl.

A pretty English cottage custom is to hang a colored blanket out the window to announce to the neighborhood that the awaited child has arrived—a blue blanket for a boy and a pink one for a girl. This custom is an offshoot of an ancient belief that the color blue frightens evil spirits. Many doors in the Middle East and North Africa are still painted blue for that reason. In Elizabethan times, boy babies were wrapped in blue blankets to frighten away mischievous fairies. It later developed that girls were swaddled in delicate pinks.

When a child is born in Savoy, all of the mother's friends witness the baby's being put into its cradle. The crib is covered with white muslin, and a bunch of flowers is put at its head. White flowers are placed on the right side for a girl. If a boy's birth is being celebrated, the blossoms are mostly pink or red, and they are placed on the left-hand side.

A red ribbon is tied around the belly of an Indian baby boy, allowing people to clearly note its gender. In China and Japan, red is the symbolic color of power. It also signals a time of rejoicing for the birth of a child.

The Stork Myth

Where babies come from has remained a popular children's question throughout history. It has proved a most fertile source from which storytellers have spun fantastical tales of birth. In China it is the Celestial Fairy astride a majestic unicorn who decides where and when purified Buddhist souls will be reborn on earth.

European children are often told that their baby brothers or sisters arrived by courtesy of the kindly stork. The story has it that when the birds fly south to Egypt in the winter, storks choose to visit the watery swamps where the souls of unborn children dwell. Upon their return, the large birds carry a cargo consisting of a swaddled babe. In Spain the storks are said to bring the babies from Paris.

There are several reasons why the white stork has been acquainted with this honor. They are known to be family-oriented birds. Extremely gentle with their young, they are also reliable and conscientious homemakers. Each year these birds return in pairs to the same nesting spot. German farmers regard the stork's presence as a sign of good luck and encourage them to nest on their rooftops. When the legends surrounding childbearing storks began, the migratory habits of birds were not generally known. Their regular absence made them ideal bearers of babies, . . . at least in make-believe.

Another possible connection is the *bennu* of Egypt. The bennu was a type of heron regarded by the ancient Egyptians as the symbol of regeneration. It symbolized the reascent of the sun, which could be easily construed as the birth of man. It is likely that Europeans chose the bennu, which closely resembles the stork, to solve the mystery of birth. Other popular fantasies have included foxes, turkeys, owls, crows, and even good old Saint Nick, who supposedly brought babies from distant Egypt.

The Cabbage and the Rose

Young children often think that a baby appears after it has been "found." Victorian parents, loath to admit a sexual deed, chose to go along with this romantic misconception. Hence it is known that baby boys are discovered beneath the blue garden cabbage, and little girls are found at the heart of a pink-petaled rose.

Chapter Four

Family Celebrations

This chapter addresses the private and public celebrations surrounding birth. Birth is a universal binder, pulling families closer, ties tighter. In most societies around the world, a ceremony or feasting takes place soon after the birth of a child. These may be spontaneous affairs, born of the natural desire to share joy. Many times, private family celebrations are planned well in advance of a baby's birth. Whatever the preparation, any such gathering is bound to be a happy and festive time.

The sequence of rites in religions is quite consistent throughout the family of man. There is the separation stage (usually a formal taking of the child from its mother); the transition period of preparing the child for acceptance (prayers or blessings said over the child); and the acceptance rite itself (such as the sprinkling of holy water or oil). The rite is frequently concluded with the bestowal of a name. This act is a formal recognition of heritage and of the child's having its own separate identity. The celebration, whether religious or a community affair, acts as the introduction of a new family member to his or her family of friends.

Family Celebrations

A ceremonial purification by immersing, bathing, or sprinkling with water is a symbolic acceptance of the child by the community. A baptismal ritual paired with a naming ceremony is commonly found in India, Greece, Polynesia, Lapland, parts of Africa, and throughout Christian civilization.

In ancient Greece a baby was given its name on the tenth day after birth. This was also a day of gift-giving and feasting for the families. In China a newborn is presented before the gods, and communion is established between the infant and its namesake ancestor.

Each religion has its own formal initiation ceremony, its official welcome to the newborn member. The celebrations noted here are a guideline for parents. A consultation with your local clergyman will apprise you of local practices and variations.

Baby Showers

Giving a shower of baby gifts is a way of sharing in an expectant mother's joy. Held by a family member or a close group of friends, a baby shower traditionally honors the mother-to-be. Today, however, it is quite acceptable to include the father and his friends in the celebration. A wonderful show of family unity and pride is presented by a shower given jointly by both grandmothers-to-be.

The time to have a baby shower is either four to six weeks before the baby is due or one or two months after the birth. Many feel that a shower held before birth is more practical because it provides the parents with much of the paraphernalia they will need as soon as the baby is born. When planning a shower, be aware that some people are superstitious and may not want to accept gifts before birth. It is best, therefore, to ask the couple in advance if this is an issue. In the case of a surprise shower, the maternal grandmother or aunt should be able to inquire discreetly.

A shower held after the birth has certain advantages. The timing allows guests from out of town to meet the newborn as well as congratulate the parents in person. Another consideration is that new parents will have had a chance to feel comfortable with their baby and will probably be eager to show him or her off.

A weekend tea or late-morning brunch is a cozy choice for

a baby shower celebration. A simple arrangement of tea sand-wiches and simple finger foods often work best.

Showers commonly have themes. This can be accomplished either with a common decorative wrapping, such as storks or cherubs, or with the type of gift itself. The parameters can be set by those giving the shower. Popular baby themes are:

Mother-to-be pampering (for example, pretty negligees, a man-icure or pedicure session at a local beauty salon, some makeup or scent, an overnight bag for the hospital stay).

Nursery accessories (such as a crib bumper, changing table, small decorative rug, framed print, baby intercom).

Baby clothes (anything from bibs to linen suits).

The portable baby (car seat, push chair, carriage, changing bag and mat).

In the case of a second-time pregnancy, ask first before buying anything major. The mother may already have it from her first baby.

Planning a
Christening

Baptism is an ancient ceremony in which a child is welcomed into the Christian religion. The ceremony acknowledges that God has created the child and marks the beginning of the child's religious beliefs. As fostered by the parents and godparents.

In the legends of folklore, unbaptized children are often cited as the preferred prey of evil witches and fairies. An unbaptized child is a child unprotected by God. For this reason christenings follow closely after births—most within six months. Every parish has its own variations of the ceremony. If you wish to follow a particular order of services or include a special hymn, it is best to discuss your thoughts with the attending clergyman.

The first choice to be made is that of the godparents. After the godparents have been asked and have accepted, the parents should arrange an appointment with their local parish priest. The obligations of bringing up the child in the faith are discussed at this meeting. In the Catholic church a series of three or four discussions concerning the ceremony are needed. The priest may also talk about how bringing a child into the world will change the parents' obligations to the church. The duties of the godparents are also explained at this time. An appropriate date will then be set, and further arrangements can be made.

A baptism is a family affair, and formal invitations are not called for. Parents usually send out handwritten letters to close relatives and friends, giving the details of the occasion. As with most invitations, these should be sent out at least four weeks prior to the date. A small tea or lunch can be served at the reception following the ceremony, but it is not required. If the baptism is to take place during a scheduled Sunday service, it is the custom of many parishes to follow it with an informal reception at the church itself, where members of the baptismal party usually bring a large sliced cake to serve to fellow parishioners. In France and Belgium handfuls of sugar-coated almonds, called *dragées*, are given out at the end of the ceremony.

A general rule of thumb for guests and godparents is to wear "Sunday best" attire. The baby is dressed in a white robe and cap. Many families pass their christening dresses down from generation to generation. In the Church of England of Victorian times, the christening cap was kept on during the ceremony and until the following morning. Some believe that children baptized under the light of the same candle will always be fond of each other; therefore, you may want to bring a large taper to be blessed by the officiating clergyman. The candle can be kept for use in subsequent family baptisms.

For those who are nonpracticing members of a Christian church, an alternative religious ceremony can be arranged. Usually called a "naming ceremony," it has become more and more popular as a base for religious introduction. A child can then choose to have an adult baptism later on in life.

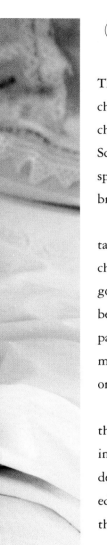

Choosing Godparents

The Church of England calls for three godparents: two of the child's own sex and one of the opposite. The Roman Catholic church requires two: one man and one woman. The Church of Scotland calls for none at all. In the Jewish religion a pair of sponsors, or *sandek* and *sandeket*, are selected to participate in the bris and simchat bat ceremonies.

Choosing godparents for the newborn is often a difficult task. It places both honor and a heavy responsibility on those chosen. Because the baby is clearly too young to answer for itself, godparents are called upon to make the proper responses on its behalf at the baptismal ceremony. In Christian religions a godparent technically answers for the child until the time of confirmation in the church, at which time the child answers for himself or herself.

In bygone days the duties of a godparent extended beyond the perimeters of the churchyard. Should the parents prove lax in their religious responsibilities, Christian godparents were under obligation to step in and take over that part of their godchild's education. They were sometimes requested to choose a name for their godchild as well.

It is common practice for the priest or rabbi to question the religious background of the proposed godparents. In theory they should be confirmed members of the child's church.

The French often have one of the baby's older siblings as a godparent. This probably comes from a wish for the newborn to continue in the family's religious beliefs. For similar reasons it is also common for an aunt or uncle to act as sponsor. In some Christian religions the godparents should not be married to each other, nor should they be the infant's parents. The Jewish faith often has sponsors who are married to each other.

The Christian godparent may be expected to present the child with a Patenbrief or God letter. These vary widely in content and in form. The simplest and nicest is in the form of a folded letter or card wishing the best possible life for the child.

Gifts are traditionally of silver: a silver cup, spoon, hairbrush, or tray. However, a christening gift from a godparent should be chosen for its lasting value rather than its immediate pleasure. A gift such as a rattle or teddy bear is not considered appropriate.

Some Godparent Lore

♥ *It is said that a godparent will influence a ninth of the godchild's character.*

♥ *If the woman carrying the child is made to look back on the way to the baptismal font, the infant will cry a lot during the first year.*

♥ *If the godfather recites the creed badly, the baby will be dishonest.*

♥ *A godparent who looks into the font will cause the child to resemble him or her.*

♥ *In Spain the godfather used to give the godmother a branch of laurel tied with braided ribbons, and danced with her after the ceremony.*

♥ *Among the Basques there is often only a godmother. She is accompanied by other women and a group of young children carrying trays of flowers in a postbaptismal procession.*

Ceremonial
Baptismal Rites

Protestant

The Protestant baptismal ceremony is beautiful in its simplicity. It is traditionally held within a Sunday service. If a private baptism has been arranged, a public blessing at a subsequent service will be made. Godparents (or their proxies) and the child's parents must be in attendance. Standing at the font, one of the godmothers holds the baby on the clergyman's left. Once the ceremony has begun, she will transfer the child to his left arm.

The godparents, speaking as one for the child, are asked to make their promises to God and to renounce the Devil. At this time the names of the child are spoken by the godparents. The priest baptizes the child with blessed water, saying the given names aloud. A cross is made with water on the baby's brow, and the child is then passed back to the godmother. A candle is sometimes lit and held by the godfather while the priest says, "I give you this sign to show that you have passed from shadow into light." A final blessing is made, reminding the parents and godparents of their committed duties to God and the child.

Roman Catholic

The rite of baptism can occur during a Mass as a communal baptism of several children or remain a traditional private ceremony. The ceremony begins with a welcoming of the child. The priest then asks what name the child is to be given. The godfather or godmother replies with the chosen names, one of them being that of a saint. The priest then asks what the parents are asking of God's church for the child. The parents answer, "Baptism." There follows a reminder of the responsibilities undertaken by both parents and godparents in the name of the child. The creed is recited by all present. The prayer of Exorcism and Anointing is now read by the priest, who anoints the child on the breast with holy oil.

When the party has gathered at the font, the prayers for the renunciation of sin and the profession of faith are said. The priest asks if it is the parents' and godparents' will that the child be blessed in the faith. They answer simply, "It is," and the baptism by holy water can proceed. The baptismal water is blessed and a little of it poured over the baby's head while the godmother holds the child. The priest says, "I baptize you in the name of the Father, Son, and Holy Spirit."

The priest blesses the child with chrism. With this blessing, the child receives the Holy Spirit. The godparent is then given a candle to hold, representing the light of faith burning in the heart of the christened child. It is the solemn duty of the godparent to keep the flame of faith alive in the child's heart. A white veil or cloth is placed over the child's head for a moment, symbolizing the Christian dignity that now clothes the child. It is hoped that the garment will not be stained by sinfulness before the child is ceremonially accepted as an adult in the sacrament of Confirmation. A final prayer is said over the baby's ears and mouth so that the child will be able to receive the word of the Lord and proclaim his or her faith.

The baptism concludes with a blessing of the mother and the father to remind them of their religious duties and to thank God for this child's life.

In recent years an alternative christening ceremony has been practiced in the Catholic Church. In the "new rite of baptism," which has been adapted for the way we live today, the parents play a much larger role. It is not intended to diminish the role of the godparents but to make it more realistic. In this new rite the parents have a chance to renew their own faith and to vow responsibility for the religious upbringing of their child. The godparents accept the task of assisting by good example. This is a departure from the classic role of godparents as sole guardians of a child's faith. Depending on your parish, this rite may be one to consider.

Other Christening Customs

There are several customs surrounding the comings and goings of the baptismal ceremony. In the north of England, two slices —one of bread and the other of cheese—are given to the first person met in the procession to the church. In eastern Cornwall the gift is a piece of christening cake or *kimbly*. In return for the food, the recipient must give the infant three things along with his or her good wishes. A *cheeld's fuggan*, or small currant cake, was prepared in western Cornwall. This was given to the first person who crossed the path of a christening procession after the baptismal ceremony.

Along the range of the Pyrenees, bread and cake protect a newborn on the way to church. The food is then given to the first person met on coming out. There is often a scramble by village children for nuts, almonds, pence, or candies thrown by the godparents into the street.

To protect a child from stammering or muteness, the godfather and godmother were supposed to kiss as they passed under the belfry on their way out of the church.

When a Basque child cries at a christening, it is considered a good sign. The cries signal that the Devil has been chased away and that the child is now pure. For this reason many godmothers give the baby a gentle pinch to guarantee the exorcism; In parts of Scotland, the north door of the church was left open during the baptism so that the Devil could make an easy exit.

In parts of Germany a large taper is presented to a baby at birth. The beeswax candle has twelve equally spaced segments on it. The marks are made by cloves or pressed-flower petals imbedded in the wax. The taper is lit briefly at the christening ceremony and then kept safe until the following year. On the baby's first birthday the candle is burned down to the first clove. Each year the candle is diminished by one-twelfth until it is completely finished, marking the child's passage from childhood.

The candle pictured opposite was bought at a church in Venice. Church candles have a singular, almost translucent quality. These molded, dipped, or rolled beeswax candles are well suited to the tradition of a twelve-year candle. To implant the cloves in the wax, bore a shallow hole with the point of a thin nail, then press the pointed tip of the clove into the wax. Be careful not to force the clove, or it will break. As the taper burns down, the cloves will fill the room with a light, delicious, tangy scent.

Baby Lore

Jewish Ceremonies
Brit Milah

The covenant of circumcision is one of the most enduring contracts ever pledged. Brit milah (also known as a bris in the United States) is at once a physical sign of the bond between the sons of Israel and God, and a spiritual contract. The ritual drawing of blood is performed on the eighth day after birth, just as Abraham circumcised his firstborn son Isaac on the eighth day. The ritual is a religious announcement that a son has entered the covenant of his forefathers.

A brit milah is the responsibility of the father. Jews following an Orthodox faith do not include women at all in the brief ceremony. Today, however, many female Jews participate fully. Some mothers prefer not to be present but join in only when the circumcision has been performed and the celebrations begun.

A bris must take place before sundown, but other than that, the time of day is not specified. Most occur in the early morning, however, because Jewish custom calls for a hastening of any mitzvah (commandment). If the child is in poor health, the bris can be delayed, but if there has been a postponement, the ceremony cannot be rescheduled on Shabbat (the Sabbath) or any other Jewish holiday.

No formal invitations are extended to a bris. Instead, an announcement is *issued*, naming the time and place of the ceremony. This way, guests unable to intend are spared the embarrassment of declining the special invitation. This family ceremony usually takes place at the newborn's home. Parents, grandparents, and close friends are in attendance. It is a mitzvah, however, to have as large a crowd as possible for the celebration of a bris.

An invisible but welcome guest is the prophet Elijah. He is represented by the chair of Elijah, on which the baby is placed briefly before the act of circumcision. This is a symbolic gesture, and any chair can be used. Some Jews choose to cover Elijah's chair with a piece of cloth that will be used to wrap the baby in. Others place a prayer book and an ornate pillow on the chair.

The baby boy, dressed in an open white gown and miniature yarmulke, is enveloped in cloth called a *wimpel* or *mappah*. The wimpel is sometimes embroidered with a Hebrew inscription, the child's name, and date of birth. The decorated cloth is then presented to the synagogue as a Torah binder after the ceremony, where it is kept until the boy has reached *bar mitzvah*.

The main participants of the ceremony are the *mohel* and the *sandek*. The mohel represents the father of the newborn and actually performs the cutting of the foreskin. The sandek, or godfather, holds the child during the rite. He is traditionally a family relative, often a grandfather of the child. The sandek remains seated for the duration of the ceremony, but everyone else stands. The godmother takes the baby from his mother and passes him to the godfather when she reaches the room where the bris is being held.

A short blessing is made by the mohel before he performs the foreskin removal operation. After the cut has been made, the father of the boy says a prayer reiterating the purpose of this ceremony. The mohel meanwhile recites kiddush and drinks some wine from the kiddush cup, giving a drop to the baby. A blessing follows, and the child is named and formally welcomed into the covenant of God. In many Jewish communities candles are lit at a bris, one for each parent and one for each of their children, including the newborn. If used, they should be lit following the circumcision. The ritual is now over, and the *s'eudat mitzvah*, or meal of celebration, can begin.

Please note that a circumcision performed by a doctor at the hospital is not considered a brit milah unless the doctor happens to be a mohel.

Simchat Bat

Simchat bat means joy of the daughter, and that is what this celebration is all about. The history of this custom is relatively short. It is primarily a product of Jewish American feminist concerns in the 1970s. However, this welcoming ceremony has developed into a full and spiritually rewarding part of most Jewish communities.

Unlike the bris, this rite of passage is not commanded by

the Torah, and therefore there are no rules to obey. Because of the lack of restrictions, the custom is wide open to individual interpretation and so varies from one family to the next. Most liberal rabbis favor the addition of the daughter's rite and may have examples of previous orders of service for you to adapt. Elements of the bris ceremony are often mirrored in the simchat bat celebration. The participation of a sandek and sandeket, or godparents, is usually included, along with the honored Elijah's chair.

The eighth, fourteenth, or thirtieth days are popular choices to hold a simchat bat. The ceremonial naming of a Jewish daughter usually takes place either at home or at the synagogue. Should you choose the latter, a service where the Torah is read incorporates the celebration. The rabbi conducts the ceremony at the synagogue, but the parents may officiate at home. Wherever it takes place, the ceremony usually has four distinct parts.

A formal greeting begins the rite, with prayers read by family members or by the attending rabbi. This is followed by the blessing of wine, with a drop being given to the baby.

If a washing of the feet or hands is to be performed, it occurs after the initial blessing. This ablution is performed as a symbolic action and represents the child's entrance into the covenant. In spirit the act is equivalent to the cutting ritual of circumcision.

The daughter is then given her name. The parents should know their own Hebrew names, their parents' Hebrew names,

and of course the name to be given to the baby. If a name with a family history has been given, then her namesake will be remembered at the ceremony. A few words can be said describing the admirable qualities of the namesake and the reasons for choice of name.

The Shehehiyanu, or prayer of thanksgiving, is pronounced along with other prayers or wishes that may be offered by the congregation. After these blessings, the s'eudat mitzvah (commanded meal) can begin.

Other Birth and Name Celebrations

Moroccan "Good Name" Ceremony

When a child is born to a Muslim family, the parents are not congratulated. Rather, thanks are given to Allah for the gift. The father of the child whispers the name of Allah into the child's ear immediately after birth so that His name is the first to enter the baby's ears.

In some parts of Morocco a communal cry of joy is given by the women to announce to the surrounding neighborhood that a birth has occurred. The cries signal that it is time to rejoice. The newborn's maternal grandmother is usually present to help her daughter at birth and again at the time of naming. The mother is fed a heartening meal of farm-chicken broth. The women then begin to prepare the sweets that will be served to well-wishers.

On the seventh day following birth, the Muslim baby receives a "good name." This obeys a decree from the Prophet. A sacrifice is made at that time in honor of Abraham's attempted sacrifice of his firstborn son Isaac. A sheep is killed and offered to Allah. The animal represents the blood, flesh, hair, and bone of the newborn child. The ritual slaughter is made on the day of the ceremony and the meat served at the celebration. The meat is often distributed among the less fortunate. This feasting and sacrifice are recognitions of the gift that Allah has given.

Once the sheep has been killed, the morning ceremony can take place and the child can be named. The men eat the mutton at lunch and the women at dinner. The male child is usually circumcised at this time as well.

Other Muslim Customs

In the Sudan a newborn baby is given a taste of specially prepared water. The water has washed a wooden board on which were written verses of the Koran. On the seventh day the newborn's head is shaved except for a tuft on the top of the skull. This tuft is left because a lock of Allah's will be seized by the Archangel Gabriel to help the child on the last day. Some Muslims weigh this shorn hair and give a sum equal to its weight in gold or silver to charity.

Another custom of the Sudan is that the faqi, or priest, conceals two rosaries behind his back. Each one has a name written on it by the father of the newborn child. The selection is then made by the mother, and a name is found. It is believed that the choice has been made by Allah, although it is customary for a mother to choose the right hand.

An old Persian custom was to write five names on five leaves of paper. These were slipped between the pages of the Koran. The first chapter of the book was read aloud, after which one of the papers was chosen at random. In this way the name of the child was selected. The name was pronounced in the baby's ear, and the paper on which it was written was attached to the baby's clothes.

A Balkan Naming Custom

This is a celebration for parents who are having trouble finding the right name for their child. The original tradition was to choose three names, usually those of elder family members. The baby was then placed in a cot with three candles beside it. Next to each candle was a piece of paper with one of the names written on it. The candle that burns the longest won the name for the child. After this ritual had been carried out, a silence of forty days was observed before the name could be announced.

A modern-day adaptation of this custom is a great focus for a family gathering to introduce the baby. The tradition is quirky enough to bring smiles to the lips of all participants and also offers a fair solution to settling any discord surrounding the difficult task of choosing a name.

The tradition also offers an interesting theme for a prebirth baby shower. A mother who cannot decide on a name will have a good laugh if she is informed at the end of the shower that the choice has been made for her. The candles should be surreptitiously lit at the start of the get-together and blown out at its

close. The tradition is then explained to the unsuspecting mother, and the chosen name is ceremoniously announced. Her only remaining decision is whether or not to accept this name of fate or to carry on with her mulling. All in all, the day will be a memorable one.

The only equipment needed is three candles, three scraps of paper on which to write the names, and a match. The candles need not be identical. A short, fat candle paired with a long, slim one will make an even race in the end. Light the candles and let them burn down a bit. At the end of an hour, gather all the guests together and blow out the candles. The one that is tallest is the fated choice.

A Planting Celebration

Ancient lore tells of birth trees planted to hold the spirit of a newborn. Today it remains a symbolic and beautiful ceremony on its own or joined with one of the other celebrations in this chapter. In many parts of Africa it is still common practice to bury the umbilical cord in the ground under a newly planted tree. With this action the lives of the plant and the child are at once bound together. In Swedish legend this tree is the sacred ash and is called a *varldtrad* or a tree of destiny. Similarly, in Russia, Germany, England, and France, the habit persists to plant a young fruit tree and then tend it as carefully as you do the newborn baby. The Swiss and Germans customarily plant a pear tree to commemorate the birth of a girl and an apple tree for a boy. A similar tradition of ancient Israel dictates that a cedar sapling be planted closely following the birth of a boy, a young cypress for a baby girl. The branches are later used to make their wedding arch. Since the beginning of the Zionist movement, millions of trees have been planted in Israel to honor a Jewish birth. (The address for this service is given in the Sources appendix of this book.)

Whatever the roots, the ceremony itself is quite simple. A young sapling, a sack of fresh earth, and a shovel are the only tools needed for this age-old tradition. In parts of Germany it was customary for the water of the baby's bath to be tipped out onto a tree or flowering bush in the garden. In this way it was

assured that the child would flourish as the tree or bush did.

All in all it makes for a fun day and a poignant first introduction of a baby to society. There are no rigid rules surrounding the custom. The festivity can take place at any time: a first smile, first word, or first birthday provides an ample excuse for celebration. A few words of explanation or prayer followed by the planting of the tree form the actual ceremony. The occasion provides a comfortable way to include a baby's older brother or sister. They can decorate invitations with drawings of trees and help prepare the planting ground on the day of the party.

A charming alternative for city dwellers is the planting or purchase of an herbal topiary. Sweet-smelling and elegant, the potted herb will serve beautifully as the living centerpiece of a midwinter planting feast.

Native American Birth Celebrations

Navahos

The baby is first fed only corn pollen, a ceremonial food. Corn pollen is also sprinkled over the water of the infant's first bath. There is also an anointing ceremony using corn pollen to mark the child as a new tribe member. The next babyhood ceremonial occurs at the instance of the infant's first laugh. The occasion calls for gifts to be exchanged as an expression of communal joy.

Pueblos

Newborns are brought outside and shown to the sun. A mother will usually choose a relative or trusted friend for this introduction. At the same time, the baby is given a name. If for some reason it is decided that this name brings bad luck or makes the child fretful, it can be changed.

Cherokees

At the tender age of four days the baby is brought by the mother to the presiding priest who takes the child in his arms and walks to the river. Facing the rising sun, he places himself at the water's edge. Seven times he leans toward the water. The baby is not allowed to actually touch the water, although it looks as if the priest will plunge it into the river. As the priest performs this action, he says a prayer to himself. In this prayer he asks for a healthy, long, and prosperous life for the child. The ceremony is completed when he passes the child back to the mother, who gently rubs water onto the baby's face and chest. If there should be a delay and the ceremony cannot take place on the child's fourth day, it may be postponed to the seventh, because both four and seven are sacred numbers to the Cherokees.

Face opening

This is one of many nondenominational Native American ceremonies that have sprung up around the country. The child is brought before the congregation at the usual weekly gathering and formally named. The child's face is shown to the people, and each member gives a simple, joyful wish to the child; for example, "I wish you flowers, because flowers have given so much joy in my life."

Honey Cakes and Tapers: The Origin of Birthday Parties

Birthday parties originally began as a protective measure against malevolent fairies intent upon stealing newborns. The theory of safety in numbers is at work behind this custom. On the Indonesian island of Ambon, the tradition began as follows: Shortly after birth, parents invited five children to a feast. The meal took place in the birthing room itself where evil spirits were confused by the presence of more than one child and so left the infant unharmed. The newborn's identity had been extended over all the children.

In the West, birthday candles are customarily lit on special cakes to salute the birthday child. An extra candle is added to the child's number of years for good luck. This custom is thought to have links to the history of ancient Greece. The goddess Artemis was honored monthly by her worshipers on her birthday. Honey cakes, decorated with long, lighted tapers, were placed in her temple to celebrate this day.

After German bakers invented the modern birthday cake in the Middle Ages, a similar custom was adopted for the invocation of good spirits on birthdays. The cake, baked the night before, was surrounded by burning candles in a kind of protective fire circle. The candles remained lighted all day until dessert time after the evening meal. A variation of this custom is the use of a huge twelve-year taper, one-twelfth to be consumed on each birthday until the child becomes an "adult" at thirteen.

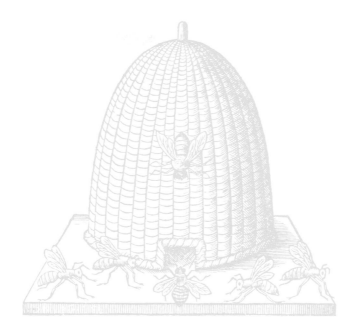

Chapter Five

Recording

Often the most prized possession in a boxful of family records is not the most valuable. Handwritten baby books are as sentimental as any bejeweled heirloom. Something as common as a collection of daily newspapers can become a birth treasure to be leafed through later in life. Recorded here are just a few of many ways to capture what a new baby means to a family.

Various mediums, such as photographs and words, lend themselves naturally to preserving memories, but don't overlook the less obvious: Pictures of a birth celebration will never conjure up the same sensations as the unmistakable scent of a sachet of baby powder. This chapter is also about keeping souvenirs of babyhood intact for the next generation to savor.

Be constantly on the lookout in family attics and even antique markets to rekindle old ideas. The Victorians came up with some lovely ones. My favorite birth record is a pincushion made of ivory silk and inscribed with a little saying: "Welcome Little Stranger." The letters are formed of the straight-pins that were used to fasten a child's cloth diapers.

the Joy

A Baby's Treasure Box

We all love to delve and rummage through our pasts. I have spent many a satisfying hour sifting through souvenirs of my childhood years, as catalogued by my mother. The heavenly smell of a nursery drawer sachet or the memory of simple lullaby tones bring us back. Collected in a splendid box they form a tangible memory of nursery days. A baby box is a sort of show-and-tell of a child's slim past. The box can take many forms: a fabric-covered hatbox, a papered letter treasury, or a small Japanese tea chest. Whatever shape it comes in, the sentiments harbored inside are much the same: Love and caring, joy and delight tumble out each time the box is opened. What follows is a sample list of contents from which to choose:

Small photo album	Hospital I.D. bracelet
Telegrams from well-wishers	Photo of baby's parents together
Photocopy of birth certificate	Silver teething ring, cup, or spoon
Bible used at christening or bris ceremony	Silver rattle
Baby's blanket	Family tree
Cards and letters tied up in a bundle	Baby booties
Birth announcement	Sachet filled with baby powder
Newspaper announcement	Instant photographs from the labor room/waiting room
Astrology chart	Hospital baby photo
Keepsake lock of hair	Video and audio recordings of baby's first visitors

Newspapers from the Day of Birth

In my own baby box, I have a collection of newspapers, foreign and local, dating from the day of my birth. They are a bit yellowed at the edges and slightly worn from my yearly leafing through them. My mother liked the idea of collecting an international sampling of what was making the world tick at the moment she delivered her children into it. She thought that the mention of a medical discovery, the resolution of a political conflict, or the start of an old country's bright new future would be hearty food for thought in future years. For parent and child, these rolled and preserved papers give a perspective on the time and circumstances that indirectly produced a new life. They can become part of a larger archive or stand as a separate collection.

Secret Letters, Private Words

When a child is born, she or he is greeted by a ready history of wishes and aspirations, ranging from general hopes of good health and financial well-being to specific and sometimes vicarious wishes such as "I hope you will one day be a great poet / doctor / banker." It has long been customary for families to keep a written record of these wishes. This tradition manages to unite two rites of passage: birth and coming of age. The letters are infused with hopes and dreams, and are sealed with wax. They are then stored in a secure cubbyhole until childhood has passed. At the age of eighteen or twenty-one, or sometimes even thirty, the seal is broken and the words are privately enjoyed.

A kind of homespun time capsule, the wish-letter holds thoughts gently weathered by the passing of years. The notes tend mostly to offer advice and direction for children who have grown to reach a crossroad in life. Their opening marks a milestone passage into adulthood and reflects all of the responsibilities that accompany that journey. It is especially touching for a child to read words written by someone who has passed away. Such letters are legacies of a lifetime of experiences. In a way they bring to life the untold dreams of the deceased.

This correspondence can be written by anyone: parents, grandparents, godparents, brothers, sisters, and friends. Some-

times a bunch of such wish-letters are gathered together and bound with a pretty satin ribbon. A thoughtful birth gift is a beautiful wooden letter box to store them in. When the box is presented after the passage of some years, it not only holds the wishes and hopes of a family but is also transformed into a wonderful coming-of-age gift.

Another safe place for wish-letters is a carefully constructed compartment at the back of an ordinary ceiling rose. Ceiling roses can be purchased in home-decorating centers or traditional lighting stores. Normally attached to the ceiling to camouflage the electrical wires of hanging lamps, a ceiling rose conveniently doubles as a letter-cache. There is a shallow chamber formed naturally to accommodate wires at the back center of the rose. This space is a perfect hiding place for the package. Once the letters are securely placed within it, attach the rose to a flat wall surface and paint over it.

To prepare the letter or letters, fold them so that they form a three-inch square, then seal the letter inside a very small zippered plastic bag. Place the packaged letter in the hollow, securing it there with a drop of heavy-duty glue. If your ceiling rose does not have an indentation in the back, cut a small square in the back of the rose with a craft knife and scoop out one-half inch or more of the foam. The rose is now ready to be attached to the wall and painted. It can be shaded with a subtle highlight color or painted in a decorative manner with the newborn's initials as the centerpiece. If the main color of the room is duplicated,

the result is more subtle and the rose blends into the wall.

A "shadow box" frame can be used for a portable keepsake. Prepare the ceiling rose in the same manner as described above, but instead of attaching it to the wall, set it on a square board or stretched canvas. A deep frame can then be built or ordered to accommodate the depth of the molding. Hung like a painting, this time capsule is one to be treasured. A series of these, one for each child, forms a unique gallery of wishes.

Bittersweet Bouquet

Drying

Tie the flowers with ordinary garden twine. It is best to dry flowers upside down in a cool, dry area. They should have at least one week

A pretty way to remember the final day of pregnancy is to keep and dry one or two of the congratulatory bouquets received at the hospital. The bouquet serves as a symbol of the endurance, courage, and, eventually, the pleasure of the birth process. A nursery door is a good place for one, either hanging from the doorknob or tacked up on the door itself.

Another less fragile souvenir is a photograph of one or all of the flowers. A photographer friend of mine snapped a beautiful, moody image of his wife's favorite maternity ward bouquet. Now framed and hanging as the focal point in their living room, it is a moving reminder of a special time.

to dry out thoroughl. In a humid atmosphere the flowe will always stay a moist. A very dry climate, however, w cause the flowers to slightly brittle.

A Family Library

A small, private library of books traces a family's history through pregnancy and birth and the sweet early days of life. A homemade record book is a very special alternative to the traditional baby book. There are several ways to structure these volumes, each having its own charm.

A *diary of pregnancy* is filled with dated notes of prebirth anticipations and the occasional moments of apprehension. The book will primarily be written by the expectant mother but can include a written commentary from the father as well. The pages recall times such as finding out about the pregnancy, how the news was broken to husband and family; the first time the baby kicked, the delicacies or junk foods that were craved, and the foods and smells that were avoided. A weekly record of weight gain can be included, along with memos of health concerns that came up during the nine months. Costs of doctors, prenatal vitamins, et cetera, can be compared. All of these can be jotted down as notes and added to with subsequent pregnancies. The pages form a richly personal reference.

A *baby book* can be made to suit your own family. Page by page, it can be constructed as a family project in the long months of a pregnancy. It presents a great way to involve older siblings. Leave space for pictures, notes, and letters to be glued in later. A pressed flower from a hospital bouquet may find itself opposite a little sketch made by the baby's older brother or sister, or a

photo of family pets. Birth announcements and baby finger imprints can also grace the pages. Be as inventive as you are personal
for the most private of memoirs.

A *baby's photo album* is a visual memory of babyhood. Pictures
of close family and friends who are important during the child's
first years are featured among its pages. Portraits of godparents,
grandparents, aunts and uncles, cousins, neighbors, pets, and
even the house where you lived when the baby was born are all
important images of a childhood. Short notes can accompany each
photograph, giving the name of the person or place shown.

Heirloom Dress Box and Garde-robe Sachets

Special care should be taken when storing ceremonial gowns for future generations. Whether a gown is a family heirloom or newly acquired, it is important that it be protected against moths, other insects, and dust. An attractive and functional storage box can be made to house the robe and accessories, furnished with a few moth-repellent sachets. These sachets, or *garde-robes*, as they are called in France, contain natural ingredients that act as a potent insect repellent. The herb-filled pouches also impart a wonderful touch of scent to the clothes.

The Herbs

The *garde-robe* mixture is put together in the same way as a traditional potpourri. All the ingredients are measured out separately and then combined in a large ceramic bowl for mixing. Less care is needed in the handling of these herbs, however, because they will not be on display. Place the mixture in a wax-paper-lined brown paper bag. The bag should sit quietly for two weeks, in a cool, dark corner. After that, the potpourri is ready to fill the sachet bags. A yearly replenishment of the mixture is a good idea. In this way full potency is assured, and the garments will be kept safe from moths. The ingredients are as follows:

2 ounces lavender flowers
2 ounces southernwood
1 ounce cedar shavings
1 ounce powdered orrisroot
1 ounce mugwort

A natural fiber fabric such as cotton or linen will allow the herbs to breathe. Cut a nine-inch by nine-inch square and fold the material in half with the right sides together. Sew down the two adjacent sides, leaving one end open. Allow a full half inch for each seam. Cut the top of the bag with a pair of pinking shears. Fill the bag two-thirds full with the moth-repellent pot-pourri. Use a ribbon made from the same fabric or a pretty cloth ribbon to tie a double knot and bow to secure the herb mixture.

Dress Box

Selecting a sturdy white dress box is the first step. Next, choose a cotton fabric with colors and a pattern that complement the material of the *garde-robe* sachet. Also have a piece of fine white muslin ready. Cut both fabrics into pieces that will cover the box, top and bottom, inside and out. Using a thin layer of rubber cement, coat the outer shell of the top half with glue, then cover it with a length of the muslin, making folds and tucks on the

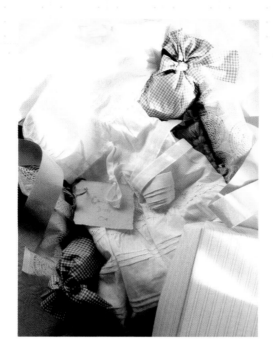

inside where necessary. Quickly press the cotton fabric firmly down over the muslin. When the glue has dried, cut away any excess that has seeped out from under the fabric.

Before placing the dress in the box, make sure the rubber cement has dried thoroughly. Line the box with a bed of thin white tissue. Use tissue to fold the dress to avoid wrinkles. A piece rolled and twisted and then placed inside each sleeve will keep them neat as well. For an extra-special touch, check your local paper-goods store for a selection of beautiful Japanese tissues. Use a couple of pieces of these or other fine white tissue to wrap the dress, cap, and baby shoes. Slip two or three of the *garde-robe* sachets in the folds of the tissue. Close the box and place it in a cool, dry place for safekeeping.

Precious Prints: Hands, Feet, and Fingers

A fingerprint is an inimitable part of a person. A page filled with the imprints of a baby's foot-, finger-, and handprints is a highly original souvenir of babyhood. This record can be kept safe in a frame, rolled up and put in a baby box, or sent to a few dear friends as a proud announcement of birth.

The prints are relatively easy to obtain, providing your child is not feeling fretful and grumpy. It might be simpler to take the prints when your baby is asleep. The materials you will need are as follows: a large plate and prepared watercolor or egg tempera paint (the most obvious choices are pink for a girl and pale blue for a boy); a few sheets each of good-quality white cards and translucent and scrap papers; a sturdy support such as a large hardcover book; a damp cloth with which to wipe your baby clean; and a patient friend to help you.

The cards are cut into squares or rectangles large enough to accommodate the prints. The paint should be thoroughly mixed and thinned with water to have the consistency of smooth, thick syrup.

Place the opaque cards next to the baby, who is supported by a flat, sturdy surface. Holding the baby still in your arms,

have your helper press one of the baby's fingers in the paint—
you may want to have a sheet of scrap paper handy to get rid of
any excess paint—then quickly apply the inked finger firmly to
the card. It is easier to bring the card up to the hand or foot.
Try to pull it away cleanly; it may take several attempts. Wipe
the paint residue off the baby's finger and then lightly blot the
card.

Next, take the imprints of the other fingers, hands, and feet
in the same manner. The translucent paper is used as a protective
layer to keep the prints clean when dry. Use a thin strip of
papertape to attach it on one side of the card.

Once you have produced imprints you are happy with, the
baby's name and details of birth can be filled in around them. It
is perhaps wise to remember that the print does not have to be
perfect. Slight smudges can be endearing, too.

Pennsylvania Dutch Name Box

A parent's gift of a painted name box makes a beautiful keepsake. The wooden box can be used to store bundles of wish-letters that your baby may have received. A larger box will make a special home for toys. It is especially pretty when painted in a Pennsylvania Dutch style. A wise move is to sketch a design on paper first.

Choose a box and paint it with a coat of primer or undercoat. When the paint is thoroughly dry, sponge a layer of thinned oil paint onto the box with a natural sponge. This will provide a soft-looking base for any decorations or paint techniques you wish to add. Include the child's name and date of birth in your design. Initials can be added to the corners of the box. When the pattern is complete and the paint is dry, coat with a few layers of eggshell varnish to complete.

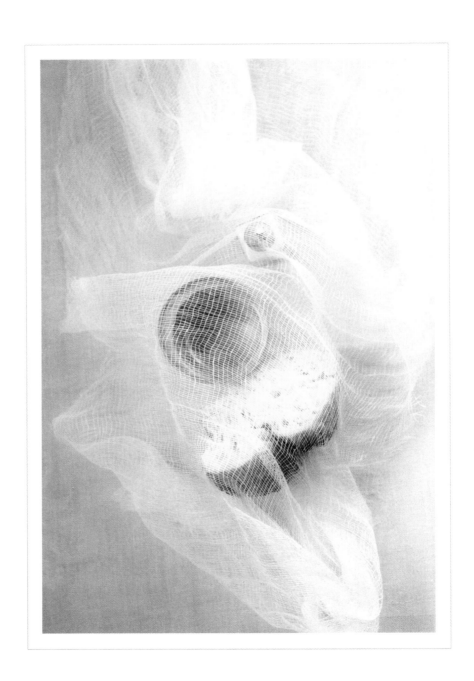

Baby Lore

118

Chapter Six

Baby Food

Many times a warm sense of family tradition is born in the kitchen. Birth and food are linked in their roles as essential factors of our existence. It is not surprising, therefore, that the two have developed an interesting history all their own.

A wealth of cultural experience can be reaped from a careful look at the food served at a family celebration. The use of certain spices or a special type of flour in cooking can often be traced to a particular inherited influence. I am not Oriental, but my mother was born and raised in Tianjin, China, and I grew up in Japan. I have learned beautiful Oriental customs that, while not of my heritage, have become a part of my life.

A birth celebration is often accompanied by an array of foods, usually including one or two unique dishes such as a traditional christening cake or a handful of sweet-coated almonds. The ritual foods of this chapter are often symbols as well as fortifying meals. There are even a few interesting customs that surround the first morsel to enter a child's mouth. Leafing through old family recipe books may well uncover a special dish that has fed a happy party in the past. If you yourself have come up with an appropriate recipe, add it to the scrapbook of kitchen memories or begin your own to pass on to your children.

Gifts of Food

Babies are usually showered with welcoming presents at the start of their lives. Some of these gifts are symbolic offerings of food and minerals to ensure that a child never wants in life and to protect the child from evil. Each offering has its own particular significance. Some of the combinations are obscure, and indeed it is hard to imagine their original significance. Here are a few bundles to present to the newborn:

♥ *The Greeks present a small bag filled with three grains of charcoal and three grains of salt. The addition of an old coin makes this charm bag especially potent.*

♥ *In parts of western England, neighbors offer an egg, salt, and an object crafted in pure silver. These gifts signify wishes for fertility and wealth, with a pinch of salt thrown in to ward off evil forces. In some places the silver has been replaced by the finest baked bread.*

♥ *A small parcel called a* weisat *is given to the children of western Germany. This gift of eggs, sugar, butter, and coffee represents wishes of luck and prosperity to the child.*

♥ *Another Greek custom is to give an object made of wood and a piece of freshly baked bread. The bread will keep the baby from being hungry, and the wood will keep the child still and calm.*

♥ One German custom surrounds the baby's first outing. Usually at the age of six or seven weeks, the baby is taken to meet the neighbors. A schwatzei, or talking egg, is given by well-wishers, and the ritual tapping of the egg on the baby's lips three times is purported to encourage early speech.

♥ A father in Bombay will pour some red rice over the top of a newborn's scalp to protect it from demons.

♥ In Serbia the traditional gift parcel placed near the cradle contains one grain of wheat, one coffee bean, one crystal of salt, a nonfolding penknife, and a cross made of yewwood.

♥ Yorkshire neighbors sprinkle a pinch of salt on the tip of a newborn's tongue for luck, during the child's first visit to their home.

♥ In northern Greece it is customary for friends of the family to bring a plate of chick-peas to the newborn. The gift signifies both the wish for great wealth and also the wish for a multitude of siblings.

♥ A Russian child will be blessed with fast growth, good health, and luck when given an egg, a piece of bread, a box of salt, and a box of matches.

♥ The custom is the same in Provence: With the gifts of salt, bread, an egg, and a match, the baby will grow up sage comme le sel de mer, bon comme le pain, plein comme un oeuf, et droit comme une allumette (as wise as the salt of the sea, as good as bread, as robust as an egg, and as straight as a matchstick).

♥ The Danes use the following protective gift parcel: garlic, salt, bread, and a strong steel instrument. These items are gathered by a close family friend and placed in strategic spots around the house prior to bringing the baby home.

♥ In the Pyrenees, the Devil is warded off with the fierce combination of fire, caustics, and foul-smelling foods. Candles are placed on either side of the baby's crib while salt, bread, and garlic are placed under it. An alternative combination is bread, oil, and salt, all covered with a pristine white cloth. As an added measure, the nursery window is guarded by the gift of wheat and coins placed on the ledge.

First Food Rituals

Around the world, the very first morsel of food to pass a baby's
lips is often the occasion for ritual ceremony.

♥ Muslims have a pious man chew a bit of
date or fig and rub it on the infant's
palate soon after birth. This action is
performed in conjunction with the **Adhan**
and Iqama *prayers being whispered in the
child's right and left ears respectively. The
parents are then assured that their
offspring has received something sacred
through his ears and mouth at the start of
his life.*

♥ *In Devon the first liquid to pass a baby's
lips should be cinder tea (water in which
a piece of coal has been dropped). This
keeps the Devil at bay.*

♥ *A common custom in both the British Isles
and Scandinavia is to wet a newborn's
lips with the sap of the sacred ash tree.*

♥ *Westphalian grandmothers put a piece of
baked apple into the baby's mouth,
believing that after eating human food,
the child has gained the right to live.*

♥ *In Herefordshire a small quantity of bitter
rue and brown sugar were pounded
together, and a minute pinch of the powder
was placed on the newborn's tiny tongue.
Bitter rue is known as the herb of grace,
and the significance of this curious custom
may lie in that meaning.*

♥ Tabezome, *the Japanese ceremony celebrating a baby's first intake of solid food, is a ritual of unrivaled elegance and simplicity dating back to the time of the samurai. The occasion marks the acceptance of the baby into its community of family and friends. The ceremony, which takes place after the one hundred and ninth day after birth, has changed very little from the days of the samurai. A small table is prepared for the baby, set with chopsticks and a bowl of boiled rice. To welcome a baby girl, the bowls and chopsticks should be red and black; a baby boy has plain black ones. The mother kneels before the table with the baby in her lap. Using the chopsticks, she places a single grain of rice in the baby's mouth. (A drop of soup or rice paste is sometimes substituted for the rice.) After the ritual gesture, the family and friends extend wishes for the baby's health.*

Christening Caudle (Eggnog)

A lovely tradition goes with the drinking of a christening caudle. The christening cake is eaten as an acceptance of the baby's hospitality. A friendship between the guests and the baby has thus been established. A cup or two of the caudle is then had by all to wish the new friend health and prosperity.

12 tablespoons sugar
8 egg yolks
12 egg whites, stiffly beaten
16 tablespoons rum
½ pint heavy cream, whipped
Freshly grated nutmeg

Cream the sugar and egg yolks together until well blended. Mix in the rum, a little at a time. Fold in the stiffly beaten egg whites, and then fold in whipped cream. Serve with a sprinkling of nutmeg.

SERVES 10.

Tante Odile's
Gâteau de Baptême

Odile's cake has graced many a baptismal feast in the hills of southern France. The recipe originated with my great-great-grandmother, who took as much pride in the presentation of the cake as in its taste. Old garden roses, pale in color, traditionally skirt the serving tray. A garland of birthflowers or seasonal greens can be substituted. It is a rich, almond and poppyseed pound cake that should be served in thin slices.

1 cup (2 sticks) sweet butter
2 cups granulated sugar
2 cups unbleached all-purpose flour, sifted
3 tablespoons dark rum
5 whole eggs
Small pinch of salt
¼ cup grated almonds
2 tablespoons poppyseeds

Preheat the oven to 350 degrees.

Grease and flour a 10-inch loaf pan. In a large mixing bowl, cream the butter and sugar until the mixture is light and fluffy. Combine the salt and flour and add the sifted mixture gradually to the bowl. Add the rum and stir well. Stir the eggs into the bowl one by one. Finally, add the grated almonds and poppyseeds, blending well. Pour the mixture into the prepared loaf pan and bake for 1 hour and 20 minutes.

Since ovens differ, the baking time may vary. To be sure the cake is done, test with a knife inserted in the center of the cake. If it comes out clean, the cake is ready. Cool it for 10 minutes in the loaf pan, placed on a cake rack, then remove from the pan and set on the cake rack. When the cake is completely cooled, place it on a plate. The plate can then be set on a tray decorated with flowers and greenery.

SERVES 15.

An English Christening Cake

In Victorian times it was traditional to keep the top tier of the wedding cake to serve at the christening of the couple's first child. The usual decoration was a tiny cradle or a marzipan stork. As with most fruitcakes, this one is quite rich and meant to be served in thin slices.

2⅔ cups cake flour, sifted
¼ teaspoon salt
1½ teaspoons baking powder
½ teaspoon nutmeg
2 teaspoons ground cinnamon
1½ teaspoons mace
1¾ cups (2½ sticks) butter
2 cups light brown sugar, firmly packed
8 large eggs, separated
2 tablespoons milk
½ cup brandy
1 cup seeded, chopped raisins
1 cup golden raisins
1 cup finely chopped citron
2 cups strawberry preserves
1 cup chopped blanched almonds

Sift the flour, salt, baking powder, and spices together and set aside. In a separate bowl, cream the butter until soft, gradually beating in the sugar. Add well-beaten egg yolks to the creamed mixture. Beat well and then add the milk, brandy, raisins, citron, and strawberry preserves. Mix in the almonds and beat thoroughly. Add the flour mixture gradually, beating after each addition. Beat the egg whites until stiff and fold into the batter. Grease a 10-inch tube pan using shortening and line it with greased wax paper. Pour the batter into the pan and bake for about 1 ¾ hours in a preheated 300-degree oven. Test the cake for doneness with a thin knife. If it comes out clean, the cake is ready.

A layer of thinly rolled marzipan or almond paste icing can be applied to the cake when cool.

Fruitcakes keep well when wrapped in wax paper and stored in an airtight container in a cool place.

SERVES 16.

Belgian Petits Fours

Petits fours are little mouthfuls of iced cakes. They are perfect sweets to serve at a birth celebration. Delicately iced in white and decorated with silver balls or sugared citrus peel, the cakes are pretty to look at and delicious to eat.

Cake

10 tablespoons butter
¾ cup confectioners' sugar
3 eggs
⅝ cup cake flour
½ cup all-purpose flour
Pinch of salt
Juice and grated rind of ½ lemon

Icing

8 tablespoons (1 stick) butter, softened
1 cup sifted confectioners' sugar
1–2 tablespoons milk
½ teaspoon vanilla extract
Seedless fruit jam
Candied citrus peel and silver balls to decorate

Preheat the oven to 325 degrees.

Butter an 8-inch square cake pan and line it with grease-proof paper. In a large mixing bowl, cream the butter and sugar until light and fluffy. Add the eggs, one at a time, beating thoroughly after each addition. Fold in the flours and salt, then add the lemon juice and rind. Pour the batter into the prepared cake pan and bake for 1 ¼ hours. Remove from the oven and

cool for 15 minutes. Turn out onto a wire cake rack to cool
further. When thoroughly cooled, slice the loaf in half horizon-
tally. Cut into rectangles measuring approximately 2 inches by
1½ inches each.

To make the icing, beat the butter until creamy. Gradually
beat in the sugar, a little bit at a time. Add the milk and vanilla,
and blend.

Coat the cakes with a thin layer of jam. This will help the
icing stick to the cakes. Using a pastry bag and a leaf tip, apply
the icing to the cakes. Decorate with silver balls or candied fruit
peel.

MAKES 40 SMALL CAKES

Moroccan Sweets

The Moroccans have a delicious way of celebrating a birth. As with most festive occasions, this one is begun by making sweets. A selection of rich confections is served to the well-wishers who descend upon the newborn's home. Like most Moroccan delicacies, this one is very, very sweet.

3 cups plain flour
3 tablespoons butter
½ cup sesame seeds
1 cup finely ground blanched almonds
½ cup granulated sugar
2 teaspoons ground cinnamon
¼ teaspoon ground nutmeg
1 cup liquid honey
Confectioners' sugar

Place the flour in a large skillet and fry over moderate heat, stirring constantly. When it has turned a light brown, add the butter and sesame seeds and mix again. The sesame seeds will turn a golden color. When they do, add the almonds, sugar, and spices to the mixture. Continue to stir for 4 minutes, then remove from heat.

Put the honey in a large mixing bowl. Gradually add the fried flour mixture to it, beating well with a wooden spoon. Taking about 2 tablespoons of the mixture at a time, roll into finger-shaped confections. Using a fine sieve, sprinkle a light layer of confectioners' sugar over them and serve.

SERVES 8.

Baby Lore

Chick-peas and
Parsley Salad

Jewish law requires that all major life cycle events be accompanied by a meal called a *s'eudat mitzvah*, or commanded meal. There are specific foods symbolizing fertility to be served at a birth celebration. Chick-peas, olives, and lentils are traditional choices. Verdant vegetables such as parsley are often served because they are also products of God's bountiful gift, the earth.

This should be prepared at least one day before serving.

1 pound dried chick-peas
½ cup good-quality olive oil
⅓ cup well-minced yellow onions
½ teaspoon salt
Pepper to taste
½ cup white wine vinegar
1 cup coarsely chopped fresh parsley

Soak the chick-peas overnight. Rinse them well and add to a pot of boiling water. Bring the peas to the boil, cover, and then simmer over low heat for about 2 hours. Remove from the heat and drain. In a large saucepan, heat the olive oil over low heat. Add the minced onions and cook until golden. Add the chick-peas and stir. Cook for 5 minutes. Remove from the heat and place the hot mixture in a large mixing bowl. Season with salt, pepper, and vinegar. Toss the salad lightly. When the vegetables have cooled, add the parsley and toss again. Refrigerate overnight and serve at room temperature.

SERVES 10.

Chapter Seven

Lullabies

Songs of slumber are songs of love. Seasoned with the dust of ages, these rhymes and melodies endure as beautiful fragments of folk history. A lullaby is meant for dreamy moments spent on an old porch rocker or beside a swinging cradle.

Most lullabies are of unknown origin. It is heartening to imagine that they cross all borders, that they belong to all mothers and children. It is believed that wet nurses brought the earthy baby songs of the land into aristocratic households. Some songs have a nonsensical, lighthearted theme, while in others the gentle cadence of repeated verses reflects the rhythmic rise and fall of a nation's history.

A babe in arms is instinctively rocked back and forth, serenaded with the same sweet dulcet tones that once brought sleep to its mother. The lullaby remains a loving melody to be passed from mother to child, to child again.

Rock-a-by Baby, on the Treetop

ANDANTE SOSTENUTO

Rock - a - by ba - - by, on the tree-top, When the wind blows, the cra-dle will rock, When the bough breaks, the cra-dle will fall, And down will come ba - by, cra-dle and all.

Rock-a-by baby, on the treetop,
When the wind blows, the cradle will rock,
When the bough breaks, the cradle will fall,
And down will come baby, cradle and all

(General United States)

The Mocking Bird

Hush up, baby,
Don't say a word,
Papa's gonna buy you
A mockin' bird.

If it don't whistle,
And it don't sing,
Papa's gonna buy you
A diamon' ring.

If that diamon' ring
Turns to brass,
Papa's gonna buy you
A lookin'-glass.

If that lookin'-glass
Just gets broke,
Papa's gonna buy you
A billy-goat.

If that billy-goat
Runs away,
Papa's gonna buy you
Another some day.

(Southern Appalachian)

Sleep, My Baby, Sleep
Schloof, Bobbeli, Schloof!

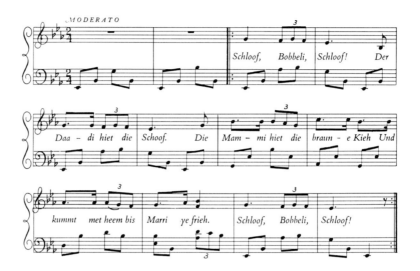

Sleep, my baby, sleep!
Your Daddy's tending the sheep.
Your Mommy's taken the cows away,
Won't come home till break of day.
Sleep, my baby, sleep!

Sleep, my baby, sleep!
Your Daddy's tending the sheep.
Your Mommy's tending the little ones.
Baby sleeps as long as he wants.
Sleep, my baby, sleep!

Schloof, Bobbeli, Schloof!
Der Daadi hiet die Schoof.
Die Mammi hiet die braune Kieh
Und kummt met heem-bis Marriye frieh.
Schloof, Bobbeli, Schloof!

Schloof, Bobbeli, Schloof!
Der Daadi hiet die Schoof.
Die Mammi hiet die Lemmer,
Noo schlooft des Bobbeli Nock lenger.
Schloof, Bobbeli, Schloof!

Sleep, my baby, sleep!
Your Daddy's tending the sheep.
Your Mommy is cooking Schnitz today,
Daddy's keeping the bugs away!
Sleep, my baby, sleep!

Sleep, my baby, sleep!
Your Daddy's tending the sheep.
Your Mommy's gone off on a gossiping flight,
And won't be back till late tonight!
Sleep, my baby, sleep!

Schloof, Bobbeli, Schloof!
Der Daadi hiet die Schoof.
Die Mammi die kockt Schnitz un Gnebb;
Der Daddi hiet die Keffer weg.
Schloof, Bobbeli, Schloof!

Schloof, Bobbeli, Schloof!
Der Daadi hiet die Schoof.
Die Mammi iss fatt uff die Blauderyacht
Un sie kummt net heem bis dunkel Nacht.
Schloof, Bobbeli, Schloof!

(Pennsylvania Dutch)

I Hold Thee, My Baby
E Hii Lei E

I hold thee, my baby,   E hii lei e,

I hold thee, my baby.   Hina i uka e,

I rock thee landwards.   Hina i uka e.

I rock thee seawards.   Hina i kaie.

My own child,   E kuu kama hoie,

Rest.   E malie.

(Hawaii)

Here Take This Lovely Flower

Here take this lovely flower
Thy mother sent to thee,
Cull'd from her lovely bower
Of true simplicity.

O place it in thy bosom
And keep it pure and bright,
For in such lovely flowers
The angels take delight.

(Shaker)

Hush Little Baby
Kay-Goo-Mo-We-Kayn

Hush, hush,   Kay-goo-mo-we-kayn
Hush little baby,   A-bi-no-gees
Go to sleep,   Wahbshkee muk-wah
Do not cry,   Kee-gah-bi-dah-quo-mig
Or the naked bear Kah kah-be-shees kos
Will eat you.   Kos-kay-be-quay-ne-gen.

(Wisconsin—Ojibway Indian)

Bye, Baby Bunting

Bye, baby bunting,
Daddy's gone a-hunting,
Gone to get a rabbit skin
To wrap his baby bunting in.

(*Traditional English*)

Sleep, My Little Babe
Duerme, Niño Chiquito

ANDANTE ESPRESSIVO

Du-erme, niño _____ chiqui - to; Du-
-er - me, _____ mi al - ma; Duermete, lu - ce - ri - to, De la
ma - - ña - na. _____ Du-erme, niño chi - quito;
_____ Duer - me, _____ mi al - ma; Duer-mete, lu - ce - ri - to, _____
De la ma - - ña - na. _____

Sleep, my little babe;
Sleep, my precious soul;
Sleep all through the night,
My little morning star.

Duerme, niño chiquito;
Duerme, mi alma;
Duermete, lucerito,
De la mañana.

(Spain)

Sleep Gently Now My Little Friend
Sov Nå Søtt Min Lille Venn

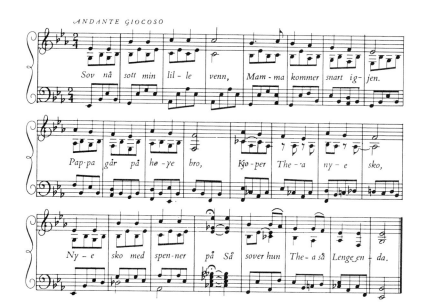

ANDANTE GIOCOSO

Sov nå sott min lil-le venn, Mam-ma kommer snart ig-jen.

Pap-pa går på hø-ye bro, Kjø-per The-a ny-e sko,

Ny-e sko med spen-ner på Så sover hun The-a så Lenge en-da.

Sleep gently now my little friend.
Mama will come back again.
Papa will go over the high bridge
To buy my little Thea new shoes,
New shoes with buckles, too.
So sleep, my Thea, sleep well,
My dear.

Sov nå søtt min lille venn,
Mamma kommer snart ig-jen.
Pappa går på høye bro,
Kjøper Thea nye sko,
Nye sko med spenner på
Så sover hun Thea så
Lenge en-da. *(Norway)*

Hush-a-bye, My Lovely Child
Fi La Nana, E Mi Bel Fiol

Hush-a-bye, my lovely child,
Hush-a-bye, my lovely child,
Hush, hush, my little one.

Sleep sweetly, my lovely child,
Sleep sweetly, my lovely child,
Hush, hush, my little one.

Fi la nana, e mi bel fiol,
Fi la nana, e mi bel fiol,
Fa si la nana.

Dormi ben, e mi bel fiol,
Dormi ben, e mi bel fiol,
Fa si la nana.

(Italy)

Ushururu My Child Ushururu
Ushururu Mammo Ushururu

Ushururu my child ushururu
Ushururu little baby ushururu

You are on my back when I grind
You are on my back when I spin
My back is sore, get down my little baby

Baby's mother will come back soon
On the donkey's back with bread
    and milk in her arms

My little baby stay with your father
Ushururu my little child ushururu
Ushururu little baby ushururu

Ushururu Mammo Ushururu
Ushururu lidge Ushururu
Sifechim aziye, sifetlim aziye
Jerbaye telate nawured mamuye

Yemamuye enat, tolo neyilet
Wetetun beguya dabowun bahiya yizechilet

Lidge dehna eder, kabatih eder
Ushururu Mammo Ushururu
Ushururu lidge Ushururu

(Ethiopia)

Bai, Bai, Bai, Bai
Bai, Bai, Bai, Bai

ANDANTINO

Bái, bái, bái, bái,
Ba - yú, Ó - lin - ku ma - yú! Bái, bái, bái, bái,
Ba - yú, Ó - lin - ku ma - yú! Shta na gór - ki, na gor - yé,
O vis - yén nei, o por - yé, Ptích — ki Bóz - hi ye pa - yút,
F tyómnam ly - ési gnyózda vyút.

Bai, bai, bai, bai,
Bayu, Olenka, my dear!
On the hillside, on the hill,
In the springtime, in the spring,
All the birds of heaven sing,
In the forest dark they nest.

Bai, bai, bai, bai,
Bayu, Olenka, my dear!
Nightingale, o nightingale,
Do not build a nest out there;
Fly, o fly into our garden,
'Neath the tow'ring, lofty eaves.

Bai, bai, bai, bai,
Bayu, Olenka, my dear!
Midst the bushes flit about,
Rip'ning berries peck and cull,
Warm your feathers in the sun,
For my Olya sing a song!

Bai, bai, bai, bai,
Bayu, Olenka, my dear!

Bai, bai, bai, bai,
Báyu, Ólinku mayú!
Shta na górki, na goryé,
O visyénnei, o poryé,
Ptíchki Bozhiye payút,
F tyómnam lyési gnyózda vyut.

Bai, bai, bai, bai,
Báyu, Ólinku mayú!
Salavéika, salavéi,
Ty gnizdá sibyé ni vei;
Prilitái ty v nash sadók,
Pad vysóki tirimok.

Bai, bai, bai, bai,
Báyu, Ólinku mayú!
Pa kustóchkam paperkhát,
Spyélykh yágat paklivát,
Sóntsim krýlyshki prigryét,
Ólyi pyésinku prapyét!

Bai, bai, bai, bai,
Báyu, Ólinku mayú!

(Russian)

Purple Straight-Grown Bamboo Shoot
I-Ken Tzu Chu Chih Miao-Miao

ANDANTE SOAVEMENTE

I - ken tzu chu chih miao- -miao Sung yü bao-bao tso kuan hsiao. Hsiao-erh tui cheng k'ou, K'ou-erh tui cheng hsiao. Hsiao chung ch'ui ch'u shih _ hsin tiao, Hsiao bao – bao, Ü - ti, ü -ti, Hsüeh hui liao! Hsiao bao -bao, Ü - ti, ü -ti, Hsüeh hui liao!

Purple straight-grown bamboo shoot
To my pet sent for a flute.
Put it to your lips,
Lips to the flute.
From the flute new music comes,
Little treasure!
Eetee, eetee,
You've learned how!

I-ken tzu chu chih miao-miao
Sung yü bao-bao tso kuan hsiao.
Hsiao-erh tui cheng k'ou,
K'ou-erh tui cheng hsiao.
Hsiao chung ch'ui ch'u shih hsin tiao,
Hsiao bao-bao,
Ü-ti, ü-ti,
Hsüeh hui liao!

(China)

Night Has Descended
Rad Hallailah K'var

Night has already descended,
   night has already descended.
Where did Daddy go? To the village.
What will Daddy buy for me?
A goat and a kid.
Who will milk the goat, who?
Both of us my son.
Lu, lu, lu, lu, lu,
Lu, lulu, lu, lu lu lu,
Lu, lu, lu, lu, lu.

Rad hallailah k'var, rad hallailah k'var
L'an halach abba? El hakkfar.
Mah yikneh abba li?
Ez achat ug'di.
Mi haez yachlov, mi?
Sh'neinu v'ni.
Lu, lu, lu, lu, lu
Lu, lulu, lu, lu lu lu,
Lu, lu, lu, lu, lu.

(Israel)

Sources

These pages offer just a sampling of my favorite nursery sources.

Baby Clothes and Nursery Furnishings

Leslie Allen At Home
Hatbox Collections
3 Kings Highway N.
Westport, CT 06880
☎ (203) 454-4155
(Mail-order service)
A selection of antiques and nursery accessories, including the Newborn Baby Collection hatbox gift.

Cherchez
862 Lexington Avenue
New York, NY 10021
☎ (212) 737-8215
(Mail-order service)
Potpourri botanicals, essential oils, and scented gifts.

Designers Guild
277 Kings Road
London SW3 5EN,
England
☎ (071) 351-5775
(International mail-order service)
Fabrics, wallpapers, furnishings, and decorative accessories.

Dragons of Walton Street Ltd.
23 Walton Street
London SW3 2HX,
England
☎ (071) 589-3795
(International mail-order service)
Hand-painted nursery furniture and accessories.

hanna Andersson Catalog
1010 N.W. Flanders Street
Portland, OR 97209
☎ (800) 222-0544
(Mail-order service)
Swedish-style cotton baby wear.

Monogrammed Linen Shop
168 Walton Street
London SW3 2JL,
England
☎ (071) 589-4033
(International mail-order service)
*Continental nursery linens, children's
wear, and gifts.*

paper white ltd.
P. O. Box 956
Fairfax, CA 94930
☎ (415) 457-7673
*Linen and lace christening gowns, bed
linens, and frames.*

Patrizia Wigan Designs
19 Walton Street
London SW3 2JL,
England
☎ (071) 823-7080
(International mail-order service)
Fine nursery clothes, lined moses baskets.

Selfcare Catalog
P. O. Box 130
Mandeville, LA 70470-0130
☎ (800) 345-3371
(Mail-order service)
*Earth Mother Lullabies—recorded
lullabies from around the world, on two
cassettes.*

Hebrew Calligraphers

Elaine Adler
3 Sunny Knoll Terrace
Lexington, MA 02713

Betsy Platkin Teutsch
629 West Cliveden Street
Philadelphia, PA 19119-3651

Birth Records

There are some wonderful ways to
commemorate a birth. The following
services provide a few. Search
through general mail-order catalogs;
there is usually a selection of birth-
related items.

Lyn Le Grice Stencil Designs, Ltd.
The Stencilled House
53 Chapel Street
Penzance TR18 4AF,
England
☎ (0736) 64193
(International mail-order service)
*Name stencil and nursery design (please
specify: cut or uncut).*

Geary's Catalog
351 North Beverly Drive
Beverly Hills, CA 90210-4794
(Mail-order service)
Porcelain plates with name and date,
and inscription on back from giver.

B. G. Genius Catalog
22121 Crystal Creek Blvd., S.E.
P. O. Box 3008
Bothell, WA 98041-3008
☎ (800) 468-4410
(Mail-order service)
Name a star: The International Star
Registry will give a name to an
unnamed visible star.

Equinox at The Astrology Shop
78 Neal Street
London WC2H 9PA,
England
☎ (071) 497-1001
(International mail-order service)
Astrological birth chart.

Jewish National Fund
42 East 69th Street
New York, NY 10021
☎ (212) 737-7441
or (212) 879-9300
Tree planting in Israel.

For Your Family Library

Books of My Very Own
Book-of-the-Month Club
Camp Hill, PA 17011-9901
☎ (800) 233-1066
Book club for infants and children.

For information about the following
publications, write or call the com-
panies listed.
Birth Ceremonies Guide and *Blessing*
the Birth of a Daughter: Jewish
Naming Ceremonies for Girls edited by
Toby Fishbein Reifman:
Jewish Women's Resource Center
National Council of Jewish Women,
New York Section
9 East 69th Street
New York, NY 10021

Children and Mothers-to-be Edition cat-
alogs for expectant parents:
The Catalogue's Catalogue
Information Publications, Inc.
308 Hunters Run Lane, Suite 1000
Mt. Juliet, TN 37122

A catalog of classic and modern children's books:
Books of Wonder
132 Seventh Avenue
New York, NY 10011
☎ (212) 989-3270

Bibliography

Listed here is a range of books to help readers who wish to delve deeper into their pasts. Some of the books are out of print but can be found with a little effort. Libraries or stores that specialize in antique and out-of-print books usually have an interesting selection of older folklore publications.

Addison, Josephine. *The Illustrated Plantlore*. London: Sidgwick & Jackson, 1985.

Alford, Violet. *Pyrenean Festivals*. London: Chatto & Windus, 1937.

Alpers, Anthony. *The World of the Polynesians*. Oxford: Oxford University Press, 1987.

Argenti, Philip P., and Rose, H. J. *The Folklore of Chios*. Cambridge: Cambridge University Press, 1949.

Blake, William. *Songs of Innocence*. New York: Minton, Balch & Co., 1926.

Botkin, B. A. *A Treasury of Southern Folklore*. New York: Crown Publishers, 1949.

Brasch, R. *How Did It Begin?* Croydon, England: Longmans, Green and Co., Ltd, 1965.

Canziani, Estella. *Costumes, Traditions and Songs of Savoy*. London: Chatto & Windus, 1911.

Caradeau, Jean-Luc, and Donner, Cecile. *The Dictionary of Superstitions*. London: Granada, 1985.

Commins, Dorothy Berliner. *Lullabies of the World*. New York: Random House, 1967.

Crane, Walter. *The Baby's Bouquet*. London: George Routledge & Sons.

Culpepper, Nicholas. *Culpepper's English Physician and Complete Herbal* (arranged by Mrs. C. F. Leyel). New York: Arco Publications, 1961.

Diamant, Anita. *The Jewish Baby Book*. New York: Summit Books, 1988.

Donald, Elsie Burch, editor. *Debrett's Etiquette and Modern Manners*. London: Pan Books Ltd., 1982.

Dore, Henry. *Chinese Customs*. Translated by M. Kennelly, S.J. Singapore: Graham Brash Publishers, 1987.

Duncan, Marion H. *Customs and Superstitions of Tibetans*. London: The Mitre Press, 1964.

Dunn, Charles. *Everyday Life in Traditional Japan*. New York: G. P. Putnam's Sons, 1969.

Eichler, Lillian. *The Customs of Mankind*. London: William Heinemann Ltd., 1924.

Frazer, Sir James. *The New Golden Bough*. Abridged by Dr. Theodor H. Gaster. New York: New American Library, 1959.

Funk & Wagnall's Standard Dictionary of Folklore, Mythology, and Legend. 1949.

Greenaway, Kate. *The Illustrated Language of Flowers*. London: Macdonald and Jane's Publishers Ltd., 1978.

Heaps, William A. *Birthstones and the Lore of Gemstones*. London: Angus and Robertson, 1969.

Hole, Christina. *English Folklore*. London: B. T. Batsford, 1940.

Ickis, Marguerite. *The Book of Festivals and Holidays the World Over*. New York: Dodd, Mead and Company, 1970.

Kantrowitz, Barbara, and Haber, Michele Ingrassia. *The Ultimate Baby Catalogue*. New York: Workman Publishing.

Knightly, Charles. *The Customs and Ceremonies of Britain*. London: Thames & Hudson Ltd., 1986.

Kodansha Encyclopaedia. New York: Harper & Row, 1983.

Langseth-Christensen, Lillian. "The Christening," *Gourmet Magazine*. October 1962.

Le Grice, Lyn. *The Stencilled House*. London: Dorling Kindersley Publishers Ltd., 1988.

Orbach, Barbara Milo. *The Scented Room*. New York: Clarkson N. Potter, Inc., 1986.

Palgrave-Moore, Patrick. *How to Record Your Family Tree*. Norwich, England: Elvery Dowers Publications, 1988.

Parker, Julia. *The Astrologer's Handbook*. London: Mitchell Beazley Publishers, 1989.

Porter, E. *Cambridgeshire Customs & Folklore*. London: Routledge & Kegan Paul, 1969.

Powell, Claire. *The Meaning of Flowers*. London: Jupiter Books, 1977.

Puckett, Newbell Niles. *Folk Beliefs of the Southern Negro*. University of North Carolina Press, 1926.

Russ, Jennifer M. *German Festivals and Customs*. New York: Oswald Wolff, 1982.

Shad, Abdur Rehman. *Muslim Etiquettes*. Delhi: Taj Company, 1989.

Sloane, Annie, and Bryan, Felicity. *Nursery Style*. New York: Viking Penguin, 1989.

Tuleja, Tad. *Curious Customs*. New York: Harmony Books, 1987.

Van Gennep, Arnold. *The Rites of Passage*. London: Routledge & Kegan Paul, 1960.

Veyrin, Philippe. *Les Basques*. Paris: Arthaud, 1975.

Voake, Charlotte. *First Things First, a Baby's Companion*. London: Walker Books, 1988.

Walkley, Christina. *Welcome Sweet Babe, a Book of Christenings*. Bristol, England: Peter Owen Publishers, 1987.

Walsh, William. *Curiosities of Popular Customs*. New York: Lippincott Co., 1897.

About the Author

Odette Chatham-Baker grew up in Tokyo, London, and San Francisco. She began her career in the photography collection of the Victoria and Albert Museum in London. She has since worked on the editorial staff of *Self* magazine and produced freelance stories on travel, life-style, and decorating in New York City. She currently spends her time in Paris, London, and the United States.

About the Photographer

Christopher Baker is based in Europe and works for select magazines and advertising agencies. His photographs have illustrated twelve books, including *The Natural Cuisine of George Blanc* and *The Glory of Roses*.